Calvin's Doctrine of the
Work of Christ

Calvin's Doctrine of the Work of Christ

John Frederick Jansen

James Clarke & Co

JAMES CLARKE & CO

P.O. Box 60
Cambridge
CB1 2NT
United Kingdom

www.jamesclarke.co
publishing@jamesclarke.co

Paperback ISBN: 978 0 227 17680 1
PDF ISBN: 978 0 227 90662 0
ePub ISBN: 978 0 227 90663 7

British Library Cataloguing in Publication Data
A record is available from the British Library

First published by James Clarke & Co, 1956

Reprinted 2022

Copyright © John F. Jansen, 1956

All rights reserved. No part of this edition may be reproduced,
stored electronically or in any retrieval system, or transmitted
in any form or by any means, electronic, mechanical,
photocopying, recording, or otherwise, without
prior written permission from the Publisher
(permissions@jamesclarke.co).

To
My Mother and Father

"Whoever does not know the office of Jesus Christ, can never trust in God, nor make prayers and supplications: he will be always in anxiety and doubt and dissimulation. Unless faith comes and shows us the way, it is certain (I say) that we shall never have access to God."

Calvin, Sermon on Luke ii. 9-14
[trans. T. H. L. Parker, *The Oracles of God* (London, Lutterworth, 1947), p. 150.]

CONTENTS

CHAP.		PAGE
	Preface	11
I.	PRELIMINARY REFLECTIONS	13
	(a) On the Relationship Between the Person and Work of Christ	13
	(b) A Traditional Formula Returns	16
	(c) Whence and Whither	23
II.	THE OFFICES OF CHRIST IN CALVIN'S SYSTEMATIC THEOLOGY	39
	(a) The Development of Calvin's Doctrine of the Offices	39
	(b) The Place of the Formula in Calvin's Thought	51
III.	THE EXEGETICAL BASIS OF CALVIN'S DOCTRINE OF THE OFFICES OF CHRIST	60
	(a) Christ in all of the Scriptures	62
	(b) The Office of the Redeemer	71
	(c) The Messiah	72
	(d) Christ our King	85
	(e) Christ our Priest	93
	(f) Christ the Revelation of God	97
	(g) Conclusion	102

IV. POSTSCRIPT	105
(*a*) Summary	105
(*b*) The Implications Tested	106

PREFACE

TWO considerations prompt this essay. For one thing, the revived interest in the Reformation is reminding the modern Church of her goodly heritage. The ecumenical movement is finding that the theology of the great reformers possessed a vitality and strength too often obscured in the later systems. It is heartening to see that Calvin studies are beginning to match the already impressive Luther renaissance. Yet it seems high time that more attention be given to Calvin's understanding of the work of Christ, for Christology is always the measure of any theology. The present essay is a modest effort in this direction.

Moreover, an essay in historical theology has more than academic interest, for a journey into the past is also a journey through the present. The meaning of revelation continues to hold the attention of contemporary theological debate, and the meaning of Christ is more than ever our urgent concern. In what sense is Jesus the Word of God? The older theology used to arrange its beliefs about Christ under the headings, *de persona* and *de officiis*, and sought formulas to bring these two into living unity. Christian preaching and reflection still have the same obligation to comprehend the meaning of the Gospel. Accordingly, to examine critically and appreciatively a formula of the past may shed some light upon to-day's pilgrimage of faith.

12 DOCTRINE OF THE WORK OF CHRIST

As to text, the standard edition for any study of Calvin is the *Calvini Opera*, which comprise fifty-nine volumes of the *Corpus Reformatorum*. The volume numbers cited below refer to the *Calvini Opera*, and not to the full *Corpus*, of which they form volumes 29-87. I have used the English translation of the commentaries, edited by the Calvin Translation Society, and lately reprinted by the Wm. B. Eerdmans Company. For the definitive 1559 edition of the *Institutes* I have used Allen's translation. For the most part, I have gone to the *Calvini Opera* for the sermons and homilies, as well as for the earlier editions of the *Institutes* and the other doctrinal works. Some of the Scripture quotations are from the Revised Standard Version of the Bible, copyright 1946 and 1952. Two indicated quotations are taken with permission from *The Bible: A New Translation* by James Moffatt, copyright 1922, 1935, and 1950 by Harper & Brothers.

This study has grown out of an interest in Calvin and Christology which was first awakened during graduate work at Princeton Theological Seminary. It is fitting to express my gratitude to Professor Josef Hromadka (now of Prague) and to Professor Otto Piper for helpful insights that have remained with me.

I am indebted to my late colleague, Professor Mars Westington of Hanover College, for generous help in checking and improving my translations from the Latin. Finally, it is a pleasure to record that the completion of this manuscript was aided by a research grant from Hanover College.

Hanover, Indiana

CHAPTER ONE

PRELIMINARY REFLECTIONS

(a) On the Relationship Between the Person and Work of Christ

THE Church's message to our time rests now, as it has always rested, upon her answer to Jesus' question, "Who do you say that I am?" The earliest Christian confession of faith, as expressed in Peter's "The Christ of God," knew that who Jesus is finds its answer in what Jesus does. The title declaring what He does becomes part of the name confessing who He is—Jesus Christ. Now Christian theology must ever insist that Jesus' person and work interpret each other in indissoluble unity. Melanchthon put the matter in a classic sentence: "To know Christ is to know His benefits." Contemporary theology is returning to this conviction.[1]

[1] Notice how a recent work in Christology begins: "We see the man through his work. For us, at least, what he does decides who he is. We cannot disassociate the doer from the deed, the action performed from him who performs it." W. R. Cannon, *The Redeemer* (Nashville, Abingdon-Cokesbury, 1951), p. 11.

More recently, Emil Brunner has intentionally reversed the order of his earlier book, *The Mediator*, by now beginning his treatment of the doctrine of Christ with the work rather than with the person of the redeemer. Cf. *The Christian Doctrine of Creation and Redemption* (Dogmatics, vol. 2), translated O. Wyon (Philadelphia, Westminster, 1952), p. 271.

In 1909, P. T. Forsyth, that pioneer of so much that is contemporary, wrote: "Theologically faith in Christ means that the person of Christ must be interpreted by what that saving action of God in him requires, that Christ's work is the master key to his person, that his benefits interpret his nature." *The Person and Place of Jesus Christ* (London, Independent Press, 1946), p. 6.

This may be a truism, yet it needs to be said, for all too frequently Christian theology has separated the person and work of Jesus, obscuring their mutual relationships. It is not necessary here to recount the now familiar landmarks of modern theology that brought "Christology at the crossroads," for this has been admirably done in Donald Baillie's *God Was In Christ*.[1] It is sufficient only to indicate how the theological by-paths have been equally disastrous for thought and piety. When "high Christology" forgets the historic person of the Redeemer, an imposing superstructure of speculation can become very remote from a living, loving comradeship with Him "who was in all points tempted like as we, yet without sin," One who became "bone of our bone and flesh of our flesh." Propositions about God and Christ can never take the place of that personal world of the New Testament where "the Word was made flesh and dwelt among us." The quest for the historical Jesus was surely right in its desire to "see the Christ stand." Yet it failed precisely because it was not content to see Him stand in the full stature of His messiahship and sonship. Dismissing what it believed to be later accretion and Christological impediment, liberal theology drew a portrait not found in the Gospels—the portrait of a "modern" Jesus, an exemplary teacher of goodness, a *primus inter pares*, a prophet of God—rather than the Christ of God. It failed to see that Jesus Himself is the clue to His message, that the Kingdom of God comes in and through Himself, that His death is no martyr's grave,

[1] Baillie, D. M., *God Was In Christ* (New York, Scribners, 1948). The phrase, "Christology at the crossroads" is his, p. 9. Permission to quote from Faber and Faber, Ltd., London.

but rather God's victorious deed. "There standeth one among you whom you know not. . . . Behold the Lamb of God." The failure of liberal theology lay precisely in its separation of the Jesus of history from the Christ of faith, with loss of both. Now the pendulum has swung back. It has become clear that the earliest records we have of Jesus are confessions of faith which do not allow us to project a "Christ without Christology." The contemporary schools of radical eschatology and of form criticism have shown in most diverse ways that the liberal portrait was untenable. And yet, as Donald Baillie aptly shows, this does not mean that these developments in themselves offer a more acceptable portrait, for the "eschatological stranger" of Schweitzer or Otto is not yet the Jesus of the Gospels. Nor is Bultmann convincing when he denies that Jesus even claimed to be Messiah.[1] Whatever may be said about the problem of the "messianic secret" in the synoptic tradition, it must take seriously the explicit synoptic question, "Whom do you say that I am?" and Peter's joyful confession which was at once accepted by our Lord.

These passing reflections suggest the force of Melanchthon's declaration. It is essential for theology, for piety, and for preaching, that the relationship between the person and work of the Redeemer be understood. The bypaths of a Christology, without Jesus, and of a Jesus without Christology must ultimately lead to scepticism. But such alternatives are neither necessary nor warranted. There is a third way. "If we refuse to

[1] Bultmann, *Theology of the New Testament*, vol. 1, translated by K. Grobel (New York, Scribners, 1951), p. 27. On the other hand, cf. W. Manson, *Jesus the Messiah* (Philadelphia, Westminster), 1946.

be led down either of the side roads, because each of them represents a false simplification of the problem, we shall then have to rethink the old problems of the Person and work of Christ as they present themselves to theology in the twentieth century."[1]

(b) A Traditional Formula Returns

In seeking to relate adequately Christ's person and work, the older orthodoxy expressed this relationship in the doctrine of the three-fold office of Christ as prophet, priest, and king. The formula owes its popularity to Calvin who first used it as a category of systematic theology. It commended itself immediately to his followers in the Reformed tradition, was appropriated into Lutheran theology in the seventeenth century, and has also been widely used in Anglican and Roman Catholic theology. Men as different as Schleiermacher and Brunner, Gerhard and Turretin, Bavinck and Newman, have all made use of it. The formula survived the criticisms of Ernesti (1773) and of Ritschl (1870). Traditional orthodoxy found in the formula not only a convenient pastoral and catechetical help, though this was doubtless its original appeal,[2] but soon built upon it an imposing edifice of doctrine which made the formula an essential category for a right understanding of Christ's work and man's nature. For example, it was popular to see in the formula a basis for understanding the Image of God in man. Man

---

[1] Baillie, *op. cit.*, p. 29.

[2] Visser t'Hooft, *The Kingship of Christ* (N. Y., Harpers, 1948), p. 15: "The doctrine of the threefold office of Christ is a typical example of such pastoral dogmatics."

was created with a three-fold dignity—a mind to know God, a heart to love Him, and a hand (will) to rule for Him.[1] Though sin destroyed this triple status, Christ as the Second Adam came as the mediator of salvation and secured, through His perfect obedience as prophet-priest-king, man's lost estate. Sometimes the doctrine was extended beyond soteriology altogether, as when John Henry Newman suggested: "It will be observed, moreover, that in these offices He also represents to us the Holy Trinity: for in His proper character He is a priest, and as to His Kingdom He has it from the Father, and as to His prophetical office, He exercises it by the Spirit. The Father is the King, the Son the Priest, and the Holy Ghost the Prophet."[2] It is fair to say, however, that the doctrine of the three offices was not intended for such speculative use but rather was meant only to express in coherent fashion the unitary work of Christ as the Redeemer. Great care was taken to insist that Christ fulfils these offices not successively (though their order may appear in greater successive clarity during His life) but rather simultaneously. Because Christ is one, He is not now a prophet, now a priest, or now a king; rather, He is always at every moment prophet, priest, and king. In every act or word of the Saviour is revealed that plenitude of grace and power which these offices formerly suggested in different persons. Orthodoxy rightly saw that an exclusive emphasis on the prophetic ministry of Jesus would lead

---

[1] This conception of the Imago Dei has been especially characteristic of Dutch Calvinism. Cf. A. Kuyper, *Dictaten Dogmatiek* (Grand Rapids, 1910), v. 3; Bavinck, *Gereformeerde Dogmatiek* (Kampen, 1906), v. 3, pp. 365 f.

[2] Newman, "The Three Offices of Christ," in *The World's Great Sermons*, ed. S. Frist, Jr. (N. Y., Garden City, 1943), p. 137.

inevitably to moralism and rationalism, that exclusive emphasis on His priestly work would lead to pietism and mysticism, and that exclusive emphasis on His kingly office would lead to utopianism and apocalypticism.[1] In the same way that the *opera trinitatis non divisa sunt*, orthodox faith insisted that the *opera Christi non divisa sunt*, else the unity of the person would be sundered.

Criticisms of the doctrine have been of two kinds. On the one hand, those who would allow and insist upon the representative, mediatorial, "official" nature of the work of Christ, may still ask whether the threefold formula is not an artificial pattern "read into" the biblical message. This was essentially the criticism of Ernesti who strove to return to Luther's emphasis on the kingly and priestly character of the Redeemer as the proper biblical category (following the Melchizidec pattern of the *Epistle to the Hebrews*).[2] Ritschl, on the other hand, objects to the whole conception of "office" (Amt) in that it carries a legal connotation not suited to Jesus, whose kingdom is a realm of love rather than of law.[3] He objects to the use of "metaphorical

[1] Cf. Visser t'Hooft, *op. cit.*, p. 17.

[2] Ernesti, *De Officio Christi Triplici* (Opuscula theologica), 1773 and 1793, pp. 371-96. I have not had access to this work and have had to rely upon Ritschl's review of Ernesti's criticism. Cf. Ritschl, *Justification and Reconciliation*, vol. 1, translated by J. Black, Edinburgh, 1872, p. 476 f. Cf. also vol. 3, translated by Mackintosh and Macaulay (Edinburgh, 1902), pp. 427 f.

[3] Cf. Ritschl, vol. 1, p. 2: "Inasmuch as even the old school has in a great majority of instances fashioned its dogmatic heads of doctrine in accordance with the fully developed ideas of the New Testament, the introduction of the three offices of Christ as a head produces, even in the old theology, an inharmonious and strange impression which ought to serve as a warning against the continued use of such titles." Cf. also vol. 3, p. 433 for his objection to the word, "office." He urges that it be replaced by the word, "vocation."

PRELIMINARY REFLECTIONS 19

expressions" in systematic theology. Others have modified Ritschl's criticism by allowing the metaphorical expressions but denying that these should be limited to the three drawn from Old Testament offices. They ask why such figures as that of the Shepherd are not placed on equal footing.[1]

The traditional formulation was not moved by these criticisms. It held against Ritschl by insisting that the work of Christ was an appointed work, an official work, a representative action. Jesus came not to do His own will; He came as the Lord's Anointed who was divinely commissioned with a redemptive task.[2]

As for Ernesti's earlier criticism, orthodoxy continued in her exegesis and dogmatic constructions to interpret the work of Christ as properly and necessarily that of prophet, priest, and king. And yet, despite her zeal for biblical fidelity, it is not unfair to suggest that orthodoxy has been content to repeat the formulas of protestant scholasticism without sufficiently examining

[1] E.g. Knapp, G., *Lectures on Christian Theology*, translated by L. Woods (N. Y., 1845), pp. 377 f. He emphasises that the traditional figures are only metaphorical.

[2] Even Schleiermacher insists: "But these expressions are not to be put on one level with other pictorial expressions, manifestly their purpose is to be sought in the comparison they indicate between the achievements of Christ in the corporate life founded by Him and those by which the Jewish people of the theocracy was represented and held together, and this comparison is not even to-day to be neglected in the system of doctrine." *The Christian Faith*, second edition of 1830, trans. H. R. Macintosh and J. S. Stewart (Edinburgh, T. & T. Clark, 1928), p. 439.

Dorner's answer here is well put: "Office denotes a unity of law and duty, and more definitely than the word calling implies an antithesis to mere private life, however well ordered, and therefore implies a relation to a common life, and the public interests of such a life which have a claim upon official activity." *A System of Christian Doctrine*, trans. A. Cave and J. Banks (Edinburgh, 1882), vol. 3, p. 383.

20   DOCTRINE OF THE WORK OF CHRIST

the doctrine of the offices in the light of biblical theology.[1]

If orthodoxy was content to retain the doctrine uncritically, liberal theology followed Ritschl in casting off what it considered the legal formalism of an outdated Christology.[2] The Jesus of Ritschl and Harnack was clad in prophetic garments but was stripped of his kingly and priestly vestments. American theology especially was loath to use what it considered a stereotyped and antiquated schema. Indeed, it is fair to say that the neglect of the "offices" of Christ only reflected a more basic neglect of Christology itself. Even a decade ago, Walter Horton could write that "there has been something like a moratorium on the doctrine of Christ in American thought for the past quarter-century."[3]

However, it is significant to observe that with the revival of interest in Christology has come a revival of interest in the doctrine of the three offices of Christ. Following Karl Heim, Walter Horton sought to express the meaning of Christ's person and work in a threefold

[1] An interesting example is K. Schilder's trilogy on the Passion, *Christ in His Suffering, Christ on Trial*, and *Christ Crucified*, trans. H. Zylstra (Grand Rapids, Eerdmans, 1938-40). The work is an odd mixture of keen exegetical insights and a slavish conformity to a dogmatic formula. Cf. vol. 1, p. 15: "For it is as the absolute and only true bearer of that triple office that He passed through the whole course of His suffering. There is no spot so small in the temple of His passion that it has not seen Him suffer and triumph as one always discharging that three-fold responsibility." Permission to quote from Religious Publications, Inc.

[2] Schleiermacher, to be sure, adopted the formula. I refer here to the later flowering of liberal thought.

[3] W. Horton, *Our Eternal Contemporary* (N. Y., Harpers, 1942), p. xiii. Writing in 1951, however, he can say, "There are signs that we may not have to wait much longer for more systematic work in theology. Christology, the central core of every system of Christian theology, is coming to concern many minds." *Protestant Thought in the Twentieth Century*, ed. A. Nash (N. Y., Macmillan, 1951), p. 120. Used by permission of the Macmillan Company.

capacity as Leader, Saviour, and Victor—a schema that at least bears some suggestion of the older formula.[1] The respect which ecumenical theology has for her Reformation heritage is illustrated in the Stone Lectures given by W. A. Visser t'Hooft at Princeton in 1947, published the following year under the title, *The Kingship of Christ*. He avowedly returns to the doctrine of the three offices as the most adequate way of formulating the plenitude of Christ's work in the unity of His person. "The doctrine of the threefold office of Christ," he says, "is a typical example of such pastoral dogmatics. Its purpose is not only to reinterpret the Biblical message in its comprehensiveness and in its diversity, but also to provide a basis and norm for the true proclamation of Jesus Christ. It is, therefore, not a speculative, but a practical doctrine."[2] In his treatment we see high Christology combined with full appreciation of the historic Jesus. His is no mere academic interest but a vigorous attempt to relate doctrine to life, as the sub-title of the book indicates: "An interpretation of recent European theology." He suggests that although Protestantism has adequately emphasised the prophetic and priestly ministries of Christ, it obscured the kingly office, and it is precisely the kingly office that is needed to-day.

Reference has already been made to Emil Brunner's new volume. It represents an important revision of his earlier position not only in the order of his treatment but also in his acceptance and use of the traditional

[1] Horton, *Our Eternal Contemporary*. His indebtedness to Heim is acknowledged on p. ix.
[2] Visser t'Hooft, *op. cit.*, p. 15.

formula of the three offices.¹ He returns to the doctrine, he tells us, because it represents a true insight of Reformed theology—its re-emphasis of the biblical stress on *saving history*. Christ is known in what he *does*. "Revelation, Atonement, and Lordship are the three aspects of one and the same reality, of what God in Jesus Christ has done, and will do for us."² In this three-fold way Jesus Christ removes something out of man's way that has prevented him from fulfilling his true destiny. This "something" is man's blindness—and Christ the Revealer turns the night into day. This "something" is man's guilt whereby he lives under the wrath of God—and Christ the Reconciler heals the rent and restores communion. This "something" is the distance caused by a sinful will—and Christ the Redeemer breaks the power of sin and creates a new heart.³

So it has happened that a doctrine which sprang from the Reformation witness, which became a settled landmark of later orthodoxy, which went temporarily into oblivion, has once again come into contemporary coinage. To be sure, such theologians as Visser t'Hooft and Brunner would avoid the speculative superstructure once built upon the formula, but they are one with the older tradition in stressing that the offices are something more than metaphorical expression in that they do express that plenitude of redemption which God has effected in Christ and which He offers us to-day.

[1] *The Christian Doctrine of Creation and Redemption*, pp. 271-321. Cf. also his *Scandal of Christianity* (London, S.C.M., 1951), p. 84.
[2] From *The Christian Doctrine of Creation and Redemption* by Emil Brunner, 1952, The Westminster Press, p. 305. Used by permission.
[3] *Ibid.*, pp. 306 f.

PRELIMINARY REFLECTIONS 23

In the light of this interesting pilgrimage, it would certainly seem justified to re-examine the formula instead of either accepting it uncritically or dismissing it in cavalier fashion. It is time to approach the doctrine both sympathetically and carefully from a biblical and historical perspective. This has not yet been done.[1]

(c) Whence and Whither

Although the doctrine of the three offices is universally traced back to Calvin, it is surprising that little attention has been paid to the place it occupies in his own theology.[2] Indeed, it is strange that so little study

---

[1] It is true that Brunner adds a brief appendix, "On the history of the doctrine of the threefold office of Christ," *ibid.*, p. 308 f. This is disappointingly lacking in historical data, however, and for the most part becomes merely a continuation of the author's statement of the atonement.

There are helpful historical surveys in various encyclopedia: especially by Krauss in *Jahrbücher für deutsche Theologie*, band 17 (Gotha, 1872); Müller in *Realencyklopädie für protestantische Theologie und Kirche* (Leipzig, 1900); Hirsch, *Hilfsbuch zum Studium der Dogmatik* (Berlin, 1937), indicates the place the doctrine has played in Lutheran dogmatics; and Heppe, *Reformed Dogmatics*, trans. Thomson (London, 1950), indicates its place in Reformed dogmatics.

The most serious examination of the formula critically is by Ritschl, but his treatment is strongly biased by his own theological presuppositions.

[2] The only critical study of Calvin's doctrine of the offices is in Ritschl, vol. 3, p. 417 f. His discussion is necessarily brief and is restricted to Calvin's dogmatic writings without reference to the commentaries. Moreover, his evaluation is strongly coloured. A brief survey of Calvin's developing doctrine may be found in Paul Wernle, *Der Evangelische Glaube nach den Hauptschriften der Reformatoren*, band III (Tübingen, 1919).

For the rest, books and monographs on Calvin are content to attribute the doctrine to him. Seeberg, *Textbook of the History of Doctrines*, trans. Hays (Grand Rapids, Bakers, 1952), is content to dismiss the whole matter with these words, "If we disregard the three-fold division of the work of Christ, which, in Calvin's discussion as elsewhere, does not prove helpful in elucidating the subject . . .", vol. 2, p. 400.

has been directed to Calvin's Christology generally.[1] It cannot be said that his Christological thought has little that is distinctive or original, for it occupies a considerable place in his own theological effort and polemic. It is the key to his doctrine of God, to his understanding of revelation, to his view of scripture and sacraments. If later tradition claims Calvin's support for its doctrine of the work of Christ, it would seem time that we undertook to see just how Calvin uses the formula of the offices. This will offer some extremely rewarding and surprising conclusions that may help us to evaluate and construct a description of the work of Christ for contemporary thought and worship.

It is this gap that the present study seeks to fill. It seeks to follow Calvin's own suggestion: "And indeed, faith ought not to be fixed on the essence of Christ alone (so to speak), but ought to attend to His power and office, for it would be of little advantage to know who Christ is, if this second point were not added, what He wishes to be toward us, and for what purpose the Father sent Him."[2]

First, however, it is necessary to look for the sources for Calvin's doctrine of the offices of Christ. In the last edition of the *Institutes* (1559), he wrote: "Therefore, that faith may find in Christ a solid ground of

---

[1] The most complete work devoted to Calvin's doctrine of Christ is the Dutch study by E. Emmen, *De Christologie van Calvijn* (Amsterdam, 1935). His book deals primarily with the person of Christ, however, and touches on the doctrine of the offices only slightly. Similarly, the recent study by T. H. Parker, *The Doctrine of the Knowledge of God* (London, 1952), while including helpful insights into Calvin's doctrine of the Person of Christ, does not discuss the offices at all. Mention should be made of R. Wallace, *Calvin's Doctrine of the Word and Sacrament* (Edinburgh, Oliver and Boyd), 1953.

[2] Comm. John i. 49.

salvation, and so may rely on Him, it is proper for us to establish this principle, that the office which was assigned to Him by the Father consists of three parts . . . they are likewise pronounced among the Papists, but in a frigid and unprofitable manner, while they are ignorant of what is included in each of these titles."[1] Thus Calvin acknowledges that the formula has antecedents but he does not tell us where these are to be found.

Indeed, the question of antecedents is rather elusive, because the doctrine of Christ's work has not been characterised by such clear historical and creedal development as is true for the doctrine of His person. After all, there were no controversies comparable to those regarding the divine-humanity that forced the Church to an ecumenical expression. Moreover, the biblical portrayal of the redemptive work of the Saviour was at once so rich and so many sided that it scarcely could be bound by any single scheme. A study of the doctrine of the atonement will show that a wide variety of theological expression could be regarded as true.

Nevertheless, it is possible to trace a fairly definite doctrine of Christ's work in terms of what was seen in the messianic name. It is in this way that we can see the antecedents of Calvin's doctrine. Expositions of the messianic name do not necessarily mean definitive categories for dogmatics, but they do indicate what is regarded as essential to the work of redemption. In a sense, therefore, a history of the doctrine of the offices of Christ will be a history of the exegesis of the messianic title.

[1] *Inst.*, II, 15, 1 (I, p. 540). The numbers in parenthesis indicate the volume and page of the Seventh American edition.

Even a quick glance will reveal the pattern of thought that precedes Calvin. In spite of the variety of expression concerning the work of Christ, there appear to be two principal avenues of thought. One of these finds in the messianic title two offices—priest and king. The other discovers also a third office of prophet. We may add that the two-fold interpretation is far more prevalent than the latter in early and medieval exegesis.

A word of caution is needed, for these expository expressions do not necessarily guide their writers' systematic presentations of the work of Christ. Sometimes they are employed only for cumulative effect, as when Justin Martyr writes: "For Christ is appointed King and Priest and Lord and Messenger and man and leader." In another place he writes: "Christ is King and Priest and Messenger and whatever else He holds or ought to hold."[1] Yet a study of the name, Christ, is still indicative and rewarding. We shall be content to illustrate both traditions before Calvin, and then to observe them in Calvin's immediate Reformation background.

(1) *Examples from the ancient and medieval fathers:*

a. Priest-King

Examples of reading the title, Christ, after the order of Melchizidec are so numerous that one can pick illustrations almost at will.

---

[1] *Dial. c. Trypho*, in *MSG*, pp. 547, 682. Such a use of titles for cumulative effect reminds one of Newton's hymn:
> "Jesus, my Shepherd, Brother, Friend,
> My Prophet, Priest, and King,
> My Lord, my Life, my Way, my End,
> Accept the praise I bring."

Cyril of Jerusalem (d. 386)
"Adding the name of 'Christ' that it might represent the kingly and priestly authority through two select men, joined in the one future Jesus Christ."[1]

Hilary of Poitiers (d. 367)
"What God conferred on those who by the anointing of oil were consecrated as kings and priests, this the Holy Spirit conferred on the man Christ, adding moreover a purification."[2]

Rufinus (d. 410)
"Christ also is the same whether of priesthood or kingship. For at first both priests and kings were consecrated with the oil of holiness."[3]

Augustine (d. 430)
"For he was anointed as king (1 Kings xvi. 13), and then only king and priest were anointed; in that time these two persons were anointed. In two persons was prefigured the one future king and priest. However, not only has He been anointed our head, but we ourselves have been anointed His body. Moreover, He is king because He rules and leads us; He is priest because He intercedes for us (Rom. viii. 24). Indeed, he alone stood forth as such a priest that he could himself be the sacrifice also. Therefore, there is an unction for all Christians.

---

[1] Cat. X, 11, *MSG*, 33, p. 676.
[2] Quoted in Thomas, *Catena*, Matt. i. 1, vol. 1, p. 10.
[3] Comm. in symb. apost. 6, *MSL*, 21, p. 345.

However, in the former days of the Old Testament it belonged to two persons."[1]

"The king fought for us, the priest offered Himself for us. Inasmuch as He fought for us, it was as though He were conquered, but He actually did conquer. For He was crucified, and on the cross to which He was nailed He slew the devil; therefore He is our king. But how is He priest? Because He offered Himself for us."[2]

Alcuin (d. 804)

"Indeed He whom He anointed was called Christ, that is, anointed. God is in man by the oil of gladness, that is, by the anointing of the Holy Spirit, in an everlasting priest and king, in order that He might save Christians who are called by His name from their sins in that He is their Saviour, in order that He might reconcile them with God the Father in that He is their Priest, and that He might gather them into His everlasting kingdom in that He is their King."[3]

Rabanus (d. 856)

"By saying 'of Jesus Christ', He expresses both the kingly and priestly office to be in Him, for Jesus who first bore this name, was after Moses, the first who was the leader of the children of Israel; and Aaron, anointed by the mystical ointment, was the first priest under the Law."[4]

[1] Enarratio in Ps. xxvi. 2, *MSL*, 36, p. 199.
[2] In Epist. Ioannis ad Parthos, tract III, 2, *MSL*, 35, p. 2000.
[3] Interp. nom heb. de div. off., *MSL*, 100, p. 728.
[4] Quoted in Thomas, *Catena*, Matt. i. 1.

Peter Lombard (d. 1164)

"He adds 'of Christ', that is of a king and priest. For 'Christ' in Greek, 'Messiah' in Hebrew, is what is called 'Anointed' in Latin; and in the Old Testament kings and priests were anointed."[1]

Albert Magnus (d. 1280)

"He was anointed moreover as a king that He might establish a new law, and as a priest that He might minister a new holiness."[2]

"However, kings and priests were anointed. But Christ is king and priest according to the order of Melchizidec, who was king and priest."[3]

b. Prophet-Priest-King

Although the messianic name is usually interpreted by early and medieval exegesis as a two-fold office, there are a few suggestions of a triple office. Some have suggested that this may go back to Jewish sources. Josephus and Philo, for example, seem to speak of this triple dignity as exemplifying the most complete life possible.[4] Apparently Clement of Alexandria is the first

[1] Collect ad Rom. 1, *MSL*, 191, p. 1304.

[2] In Ev. Matt. xvi. 16, *B. Alberti Magni Opera Omnia*, Paris, 1890-9, v. 20, p. 637.

[3] In Ev. Lucae ii. 11, *Opera*, vol. 22, p. 207.

[4] So Josephus sums up the life of John Hyrkanus: "He was certainly a very happy man, afforded no occasion to have any complaint made of fortune of his account. He it was who alone had three of the most desirable things in the world—the government of his nation, and the high priesthood, and the gift of prophecy." *Wars of the Jews*, I. 3, in *Works of Josephus*, trans. Whiston (Phila., 1857), p. 147.

In this same sense of a full life, Philo speaks of Moses as King, Lawgiver, High Priest, and Prophet—and excelled in each of these offices. Cf. *Life of Moses*, II, 1, in *The Works of Philo Judaeus*, trans. C. D. Yonge (London, Bohn, 1855), vol. 3, p. 75.

30 DOCTRINE OF THE WORK OF CHRIST

to speak of a prophetic anointing. Prior to the Reformation, however, there would seem to be only a few instances where the three offices are related organically in a messianic sense.

Eusebius (d. 339)

"The following, moreover, is the substance of this matter, that of all who in former times were consecrated with holy oil as type, whether of priests or kings or prophets, no one until now received such power of divine virtue as our Saviour and Lord Jesus demonstrates, who is the only and true Christ (Anointed One). . . . So that all these have reference to the true Christ, the divine and heavenly word, the only high priest of all men, the only king of all creation, and the Father's supreme prophet of prophets."[1]

Chrysostum (d. 407)

"Also because Christ was to have three dignities: King, Prophet, Priest; but Abraham was prophet and priest. . . . David was king and prophet, but not priest. Thus He is expressly called the son of both, that the three-fold dignity of His forefathers might be recognised by hereditary right in Christ."[2]

Petrus Chrysologus (d. 450)

"He was called 'Christ' by anointing, and 'Jesus' by name because He poured Himself forth on those anointed with the full plenitude of the Spirit of

---

[1] Hist. eccl. I, 3, *MSG*, 20, pp. 72 f.
[2] Quoted in Thomas, *Catena*, Matt. i. 1.

PRELIMINARY REFLECTIONS 31

divinity which in former times had been gathered together through kings, prophets, and priests, into one person, this king of kings, priest of priests, prophet of prophets. . . ."[1]

Thomas Aquinas (d. 1274)
"As stated above . . . other men have this or that grace bestowed on this or that one, but Christ, as being Head of all, has the perfection of all graces. Wherefore, as to others, one is a lawgiver, another is a priest, another is a king; but all these concur in Christ as the fount of all grace."[2]

Appearing as this does in the framework of Thomas's theological system, we may say that Thomas comes closest to a use of the formula as a theological method. It is safe to say that Calvin had this passage in mind when he speaks of the formula as being "pronounced among the Papists."[3] Yet with Thomas it is still a passing suggestion.[4] The discussion of Christ's mediatorial work which immediately follows this

[1] Sermo 59, *MSL*, 52, p. 363.

[2] *Summa*, Part III, 1st no. Q22, art. 1. trans. Fathers of Eng. Dominican Province (London, 1911-25).

[3] The question of Calvin's knowledge and use of Thomas has received fresh treatment by Dr. G. A. Barrois of Princeton Theological Seminary, who concludes that Thomas's influence upon Calvin is considerable. Opposed to this view was that of A. Pierson, who held that Calvin did not know Aquinas's work. Pierson's work, however, is based on critical exaggeration and by a blind opposition to Calvin. Cf. *Studien over J. Kalvijn* (Amsterdam, 1883), p. 7, and *Nieuwe Studien over J. Kalvijn* (Amsterdam, 1883).

[4] To be sure, later interpreters of Thomas often use the scheme to exposit the *Summa*. Cf. Berthier, *A Compendium of Theology*, trans. S. Raemers (St. Louis, 1931), vol. 1, p. 321.

passage in Aquinas is wholly in terms of the priestly office.

It is apparent that the exegesis of the messianic name in the Western Church is predominantly in terms of a two-fold office.[1]

(2) We turn now to the immediate *Reformation context of Calvin's doctrine*:

a. *Priest-King*

The usual exegesis of the word "Christ" again sees the two-fold dignity of priest and king. In discussing the work of redemption, however, I think it is fair to say that the Reformers place greater emphasis upon the kingly aspect of redemption, even though they continue to stress priestly satisfaction. This is clearly seen in their understanding of atonement. The Cross becomes not only a priestly sacrifice but a regal victory over Satan, sin, and death. Aulen would call this a return to the "classic" theory.[2]

The two-fold office receives its clearest expression in Luther's *Christian Liberty* (1520):

"But that we may look more deeply into that grace which our inward man has in Christ, we must consider that in the Old Testament God sanctified to

---

[1] Knapp suggests that there are traces of the triple office in Theodoret. It is suggested also that the triple division finds common use in the Greek and Russian Church (cf. McClintock and Strong, *Cyclopaedia*, v. 2, p. 263). All agree it does not come into general use in the Western Church.

[2] Aulen is very one-sided, however, in holding that Luther alone recovers the classic view of atonement as a regal victory. Cf. *Christus Victor*, trans. Hebert (London, 1931), p. 139.

PRELIMINARY REFLECTIONS 33

Himself every firstborn male, and the birth-right was highly prized, having a two-fold honour, that of priesthood, and that of kingship. For the first-born brother was priest and lord over all the others, and was a type of Christ, the true and only First-born of God and the Virgin Mary, and true King and Priest, not after the fashion of the flesh and of the world. . . . Now, just as Christ by his birth-right obtained these two prerogatives, so He imparts them to and shares them with every one who believes on Him according to the law of the aforesaid marriage, by which the wife owns whatever belongs to the husband. Hence we are all priests and kings in Christ, as many as believe on Christ. . . ."[1]

One could add any number of illustrations from Luther's writings.[2] His interpretation of the messianic

---

[1] In *Works of Martin Luther*, Holman ed. (Philadelphia, 1915), vol. 2, p. 323.

[2] Cf. *Table Talk*, trans. W. Hazlitt (London, 1857), No. 190, p. 82: "Christ, our High-Priest, is ascended into heaven and sits on the right hand of God the Father, where, without ceasing, He makes intercession or us (Rom. 8) where St. Paul, with very excellent, glorious words, pictures Christ to us; as in His death, He is a sacrifice offered up for sins; in His resurrection, a conqueror; in His ascension, a king; in making mediation and intercession, a high-priest. For, in the law of Moses, the high-priest only went into the Most Holiest to pray for the people. Christ will remain a priest and king, though He was never consecrated by any papist bishop or greased by any of those shavelings; but He was ordained and consecrated by God Himself, and anointed. . . ."
Luther's exegesis of the title appears again in his *Kirchenpostille*, 3 Advent zu Matt. xi. 4 f, *W. A.* X/I, 2, pp. 152 f, where he says: "For 'Christ' is Greek, 'Messiah' is Hebrew, 'anointed' is Latin, and 'Gesalbeter' is German, and the King and Priest were anointed to kingship and priesthood. But this anointed king and priest, Isaiah says, God Himself will anoint, not with material oil, but with the Holy Ghost, who rests upon Him."

c

34   DOCTRINE OF THE WORK OF CHRIST

title is consistently a two-fold office.¹ And this dignity which is His by right He gives to His people by grace.

Melanchthon does not appear to make any systematic use of the offices in his *Loci*, where his treatment is almost wholly in terms of Christ's priestly work. We can find a clear statement of his understanding of the messianic title in his *Annotations on the Gospels*. Of Peter's confession in Matt. xvi. 16, Melanchthon writes:

"This whole person, in whom are the two natures, is the Messiah, that is, our King and High Priest. *Insofar as He is a Priest he has these duties:* (1) He preaches the gospel. (2) He offers a sacrifice for us. (3) He always prays for us, in His passion and afterward, nay more, from the beginning to end, according to the saying in Ps. ii, 'ask of me, etc.'

---

[1] Brunner, in his *Doct. of Creation and Redemption*, p. 314, holds that the doctrine of the three offices was not unknown to Luther, and he appeals to Th. Harnack, *Luther's Theologie mit besonderer Beziehung auf seine Versöhnungs und Erlösungslehre*, Zweite Abtheilung (Erlangen, 1886), in which Harnack includes a chapter on the three-fold office, suggesting that, while the doctrine does not enter Lutheran dogmatics until Gerhard, the seeds of the formula are in Luther himself (cf. pp. 269 f.). Th. Harnack is not convincing, however, for the very examples he uses prove rather Luther's fondness for the two-fold understanding. For example, he quotes from Luther's sermon on Ps. cx, but has to admit that Luther here subsumes the prophetic under the priestly office (p. 270). Of course Luther will call Christ "Doctor und Lehrer," but he will immediately contrast Jesus to Moses (p. 272). Similarly, commenting on Mal. iv. 2 and Ps. xix. 5, Luther will say that "The prophets are the stars and moon, while Christ is the sun" (cf. p. 273). To be sure, Luther often speaks of Christ as Shepherd and Teacher, but the teaching belongs under His priestly office, for the three functions of priesthood are "preaching, sacrificing, and praying" (p. 277); and again the word of the shepherd is His sceptre of royalty. How strange, Luther will comment, that this Shepherd-King carries us so that we may lie on His shoulders and not under his feet (p. 283).

In other words, while Luther's thought may be arbitrarily arranged under the three-fold formula, the formula itself is not native to his thought and does not express his own exegesis. The classic statement in his *Christian Liberty* ought to be proof enough.

(4) Moreover, He has the office of blessing, and He blesses not only by announcing the remission of sins, but also by the fact that He actually destroys sin and death, He restores life, since He is the living Word of the eternal Father.

He is King. Since He releases us from sin, death, and the devil, He destroys the kingdom of the devil and restores to us justice and eternal life. He is such a king, restoring an eternal kingdom, not political but such that at a fixed time He becomes the victim, as the prophet says, since He poured out His soul for sin, He shall see His aged seed.

All these things are included in the confession of Peter."[1]

This is not to say that Melanchthon relates these two offices systematically, and in this he is not alone.[2]

Both in his exegetical and dogmatic work, Bullinger consistently holds a two-fold office of Christ. For example, in his commentary on Luke ii. 11, he writes:

"We have been the servants of Satan: but, being delivered by the Kindness of Christ, we have been

[1] C. R. 12, pp. 389-90. Notice that he includes teaching under the priestly office. In his treatment of Psalm ii, however, he seems to include it under the kingly office. "Postillae," in C. R. 24, p. 137. Like Luther, he sees in the word of Christ both priestly concern and regal claim.

[2] The work of salvation is a unitary work, and its exposition frequently becomes a compilation of metaphors rather than a systematic and analytical use of offices. Cf. Zwingli: "So Christ is made known, who satisfied the conditions of divine justice for us. And thus, when He is believed in, salvation comes. For He is the guarantee unfailingly of the mercy of God.... Teaching the same thing in many other metaphors, as everyone knows, that He is our light, salvation, leader, shepherd, father, everything." De Vera et Falso Rel. Comm., C. R. 90, pp. 695, 696.

made the servants of our Lord Jesus Christ; nay, we are all brothers of Christ now and sons of God. Christ is the anointed one. Kings and priests used to be anointed. Therefore Christ is king and priest of the people of God, redeemer, messenger, defender, lawgiver, avenger, leader, intercessor, sacrifice, satisfaction, light, sanctification, life, and every good. All these things God proclaims in Christ, as He says 'There is born to us a Saviour who is Christ the Lord,' and He shows us fully what benefit we have in meditating on His nativity . . . and He says that Jesus is Christ, the Saviour of the world, the only king and priest."[1]

Such illustrations are sufficient to indicate that in Calvin's immediate reformation background, the messianic office of the Redeemer is usually understood as the two-fold work of king and priest. The principal difference between the reformers and the schoolmen lies in the more dynamic character that the biblical categories assume as they are freed from the more speculative discussions on the necessity of the incarnation, etc. Also, we find the motif of the kingly conquest frequently used to describe the atonement of the cross.[2]

b. Prophet-Priest-King

Prior to Calvin it would appear that the only reformation suggestion of the triple office comes from Osiander:

[1] In *Luculentum et sacrosanctum Euangeliu domini nostri Iesu Christi secundum Lucam Commentariorum*, lib. IX, per H. Bullingerum, Tiguri, 1546.

[2] A striking example is Farel's description of the "battle of Golgotha" in his *Du Vray Usage de la Croix*, XXX, ed. (Geneva, 1865), p. 71.

"Moreover we must understand this of His office that He is Christ, that is, Master, King, and High Priest. For as Christ means anointed, and only prophets, kings, and priests were anointed, so one sees that all three offices apply to Him: the prophetic office, for He only is our teacher and master (Matt. xxiii. 8), the kingly authority, for He rules forever in the house of Jacob (Luke i. 32), and the priestly office, for He is a priest forever according to the order of Melchizidec (Ps. cx. 1). That is now His office, that He may be our wisdom, righteousness, sanctification, and redemption, as Paul testifies (1 Cor. i. 30)."[1]

Calvin was acquainted with Osiander's principal writings and combated them vigorously, both for his speculations on the necessity of incarnation and for his views on justification. Whether he was acquainted with this passage we have no way of knowing. In any case, it is not necessary to posit any dependence upon it, because Calvin speaks only of "papists" who anticipate the doctrine.

It is well known, of course, that the Heidelberg Catechism and the other Reformed symbols of the

[1] Schirmschrift zum Augsburger Reichstag, 1530, quoted in Gussmann, *Quellen und Forschungen zur Geschichte des Augsburgischer Glaubensbekenntnisses*, I/1 (Berlin, 1911), p. 302.

Dorner suggests that the three offices also appears in the Brentzian catechism. I was not able to find Brentius's first catechism of 1527, but his later catechism of 1551 mentions only the two offices under the messianic name. This is to be expected, for he was strongly influenced by Luther. In his *Apologiae Confessionis*, moreover, he seems to include the prophetic office under the kingly. "And He has a spiritual sceptre, which is the Gospel, that from Zion governs the Church in the whole universe through the Holy Spirit." *Opera*, VIII (Tübingen, 1576-90), p. 377.

38 DOCTRINE OF THE WORK OF CHRIST

sixteenth century use the formula of the three offices in their dogmatic structure, for these are written after Calvin's *Institutes* of 1559, and simply build upon it. So it is hardly surprising to find Viret using the formula in his *Instruction Chretienne*, published in the year of Calvin's death.[1]

This glance at antecedents is enough to indicate that there are two traditional readings of the messianic name, the more prevalent one embracing a two-fold office. Calvin had access to both traditional interpretations, and we shall find that he moves from one to the other. His importance lies not in inventing a formula, but rather in the systematic use he will suggest for it. We have now to discover which of these two traditions is the truer expression of Calvin's own thought.

[1] Cf. his "Exposition familiere des principaux poincts du Catechisme et la doctrine Chretienne," Dial. 9, in *Instruction Chretienne*, tome I, (Geneva, 1564), pp. 44 f. It is interesting to note, however, that Viret admits some difficulty in properly distinguishing the prophetic office. When the catechumen asks whether the work of teaching is not properly included under the office of priest, since it is suggested earlier as a priestly work, the reply is, True enough, but since priesthood is understood particularly according to Melchizidec, as a work of prayer and sacrifice, it is helpful and needful to posit a separate office.

We have noticed already, and will notice continually, that the teaching office has difficulty in standing alone.

CHAPTER TWO

THE OFFICES OF CHRIST IN CALVIN'S SYSTEMATIC THEOLOGY

SINCE the doctrine of the three offices as a category of systematic theology derives from Calvin, it is well to begin by considering its place in Calvin's own formulated theology. Two questions confront us here: first, how does he arrive at the doctrine, and secondly, what place does the formula play in his own theological thought. While the first question has received some notice,[1] the second has not received any attention.

(a) *The Development of Calvin's Doctrine of the Offices*

The first edition of the *Institutes* (1536) speaks only of a two-fold messianic unction:

"We also believe that He is Christ, that is, filled with all the gifts of the Holy Spirit. These are spoken of as oil because without them we languish dry and barren. And we believe that the Spirit rested upon Him in such a way that it shed itself completely in Him, and that we, who through faith are His co-heirs and partners, receive all things from His fulness. Accordingly, we believe that by this anointing He

[1] Cf. Ritschl, *op. cit.*, vol. 3, pp. 417 f.; Schweizer, *Die Glaubenslehre der Evangelisch-Reformirten Kirche* (Zurich, 1847), pp. 42 f.; Doumergue, *Jean Calvin* (Lausanne, 1910), vol. 4, pp. 224 f.; Wernle, *Der Evangelische Glaube nach dem hauptschriften der Reformatoren*, III (Tübingen, 1919), pp. 42 f.

was appointed king by the Father to subdue unto Himself all power in heaven and in earth that we might be kings in Him, having power over the devil, sin, death, and hell. Again, we believe that He was appointed priest to placate and conciliate the Father for us, that in Him we might be priests, offering prayers to the Father, thanksgivings, ourselves and all we have, through His intercession and mediation."[1]

It is interesting to notice that this passage finds almost an exact parallel in his *Instruction in Faith* (1537).[2] We notice at once that Calvin's treatment of the messianic office follows here the prevalent tradition of the double unction so characteristic of early and medieval exegesis, and closely parallels Luther's exposition in *Christian Liberty*. Calvin means to include the whole redemptive work under these two offices. As in Luther, this double birth-right Christ shares with His believers. Moreover, the two offices are directly related to the atonement which is at once a priestly sacrifice and a kingly conquest. To be sure, the *Institutes* of 1536 also speaks of Christ as our Magister (Teacher),

[1] C. O. 1, p. 68.
[2] "The title 'Christ' signifies that through unction He has been fully endowed with all the graces of the Holy Spirit. These graces are called 'oil' in the Scripture, and rightly so, because without them we fall as dry and barren branches. Now through such an unction the Father has constituted Him King in order that He subject unto himself all power in heaven and on earth, to the end that we too may become kings in Him, having dominion over the devil, sin, death, and hell. Secondly, God has constituted Him Priest in order to satisfy the Father for us and to reconcile Him through His sacrifice, to the end that in Him we too might become priests, offering to the Father prayers, thanksgivings, ourselves, and all things of ours, having Him as our intercessor and mediator." From *John Calvin's Instruction in Faith*, translated and edited by Paul T. Fuhrmann, copyright 1949, by W. L. Jenkins, p. 47. Used by permission. [Cf. *C. O.* 22, p. 53. The Latin text is in *C. O.* 5, p. 338.]

THE OFFICES OF CHRIST 41

but this is not seen as a separate messianic office for it is somehow embraced under the two messianic offices.[1]

In the edition of 1539, however, the prophetic office of Christ begins to appear, though it is not yet explicitly added to the other two:

> "The name 'Christ' is added, which, though not inappropriately attributed to others, is none the less His by a peculiar right. For the Lord anoints all on whom He sheds the grace of His Spirit. And there is no one faithful, nor has there been any, whom He did not fill with His unction. Therefore it is accomplished that all the faithful were anointed. The prophets have their own unction also, and the kings have it, and the priests, not in the manner of outward ceremony but spiritually. Thus it is agreed that a prophet, who is the interpreter of God among men, is endowed and equipped with the peculiar gift of the Spirit. Similarly, it is agreed that also a priest, who ought to be a messenger of the Lord, is thus endowed and equipped (Mal. ii. 7). Lastly, it is agreed that a king also, who bears the image of divine majesty on earth, is similarly endowed and equipped. Therefore the oil whereby prophets as well as priests and kings were consecrated was not a useless symbol but a sacrament of His true and unique anointing. . . . Moreover, in this anointing He was established as king by the Father to bring into subjection to Himself all power in heaven and

---

[1] Thus in the Lord's prayer we receive "a rule of praying from the chief teacher, Christ, whom the Father has made our teacher." *C. O.* 1, p. 99.

earth, as the second psalm teaches (v. 6); and He was consecrated as priest to perform the function of intercession with the Father."[1]

This passage represents an interesting transition in Calvin's doctrine. The three offices of prophet, priest, and king are suggested as forming our heritage by grace. The prophetic office, however, is not yet directly related to the messianic name.

In the edition of 1545, Calvin has come to a clear statement of the three offices of Christ. At the close of the section dealing with the kingdom and priesthood which Christ has won for us, the *Institutes* now adds:

". . . or an interpreter of the divine counsel in order that He might discharge this office; with the Spirit's anointing He was also installed in the office of the chief prophet, from whose mouth we might learn perfect wisdom."[2]

The change is also reflected in the Catechism of 1543 (French edition) and 1545 (Latin edition), as the messianic title is now explained:

"By this title is clearly declared His office. He was anointed by the heavenly Father to be ordained as King, Priest or Sacrifice, and Prophet."[3]

Ritschl also calls attention to a change of emphasis in the kingly office. Whereas earlier Calvin saw the kingly office as verifying itself in our assurance of salvation,

[1] *C. O.* 1, pp. 513, 515. [2] *C. O.* 1, p. 515. [3] *C. O.* 6, p. 19.

he now interprets it as Christ's spiritual reign over the community of believers. I do not believe that Ritschl is warranted in saying that this "represents an inconsistency with the view he had otherwise expounded,"[1] since it does not supplant but merely supplements the earlier emphasis.

We come now to the final edition of the *Institutes* in 1559. Here Calvin adds a separate chapter on the three offices, prefacing it with a remark by Augustine that Christ is to be found among many in name only, without proper knowledge of what the name implies. Therefore, he continues, "that faith may find in Christ a solid ground of salvation, and so may rely on Him, it is proper for us to establish this principle, that the office which was assigned to Him by the Father consists of three parts."[2] It is seen that the offices are again derived from the messianic name: "Hence the celebrated title of 'Messiah' was given to the promised Mediator. But though I confess that He was called 'Messiah' with particular reference to His Kingdom . . . yet the prophetical and sacerdotal unctions have their respective places, and must not be neglected by us."[3]

The prophetic unction, as also the kingly and priestly, are Christ's as Head of the body of believers and so continues in them, "that the preaching of the gospel might continually be attended with the power of the Spirit."[4] It also assures us "that all the branches of perfect wisdom are included in the system of doctrine which He has given us."[5]

---

[1] Ritschl, *op. cit.*, vol. 3, p. 420. His objection is that this makes for ecclesiasticism.

[2] *Inst.*, II.15.2 (I, 542).   [3] *Ibid.*   [4] *Ibid.*   [5] *Ibid.* (I, 543).

44 DOCTRINE OF THE WORK OF CHRIST

The kingly office may be described as the divine guarantee of the eternity and power given to both church and individual believer. "Whence we infer that He reigns rather for us than for Himself, and that both internally and externally; that being replenished, as far as God knows to be necessary for us, with the gifts of the Spirit, of which we are naturally destitute, we may perceive from these first-fruits that we are truly united to God, in order to our perfect happiness; and in the next place, that, depending on the power of the same Spirit, we may not doubt of being always victorious over the devil, the world, and every kind of evil."[1]

As our Priest, Christ makes us acceptable to God by His holiness, appeases God's wrath by His sacrifice, and intercedes for us eternally. Calvin's emphasis is again that this priesthood is *for* us in such a way that it recovers our own, "to associate us with Himself in so great an honour."[2]

How shall we account for this change from a two-fold to a three-fold understanding of the messianic work of Christ?[3] The change is apparently not due to an influence from without, because our preceding discussion has

[1] *Inst.*, II.15.4 (I, p. 545).
[2] Ritschl holds that this whole presentation "marks a change for the worse in this respect, that the practical bearing of the Kingship and Priesthood of Christ, in the transference of these attributes to believers, has disappeared." V. 3, p. 419. This is hardly true, however, for Calvin still stresses that Christ in His offices transfers these gifts to His own. Ritschl's objection seems to be lodged not so much against the three offices as such, but rather against the objective character of Calvin's theology as a whole.
[3] It is strange that this problem has not received the attention it deserves. Doumergue points to the importance the change must have held for Calvin, but does not indicate what this must be (*op. cit.*, pp. 224 f. n.). Krauss contents himself with observing that Calvin made the change with clear recognition of its consequences (*op. cit.*, p. 598).

shown that Calvin was acquainted with both traditional expositions of the messianic name. The question of sources is important for our historical understanding of the doctrine, but it does not help us here. Why Calvin changed from one tradition to another can only be explained within the context of his own thought.

It has been suggested that Calvin made the change for exegetical reasons,[1] but the next chapter will indicate that this is not so. The three-fold office is for Calvin a dogmatic, not an exegetical category. Now then, if neither borrowing nor exegesis can account for the change, how shall we account for it? One reason doubtless lies in the conceptual character of Calvin's thought that seeks in any problem a principle of unity. Here the problem is to relate the revelatory character of Christ's work to His kingly and priestly functions. Calvin seeks to express this in the formula of the three offices. It is precisely this sense of wholeness that commended the formula to later writers.[2]

Let me suggest another reason. Calvin is anxious to find an adequate biblical foundation for the church's ministry that will preserve the principle of the priesthood of all believers while yet safeguarding the ministerial order against a Roman denial of its authenticity

[1] So Emmen, *op. cit.*, p. 51: "A description of the offices of Christ meant for Calvin no mere appendage added because of tradition. For the first time he sought thus to see the prophetical meaning of the Old Testament anointing in the concrete figure of Jesus Christ." Yet we shall see that the category never enters into his own exegetical writings.

[2] Cf. Franks, *A History of the Work of Christ in its Ecclesiastical Development* (London, 1918), vol. 1, p. 430: "This doctrine, the really characteristic Protestant doctrine of the work of Christ, is highly synthetic in character. It has not merely the value of presenting the whole work of Christ in a single view, but also of presenting it in such a manner that it shows how it terminates in the production of faith through the Gospel. It is thus of an eminently practical character."

and an Anabaptist repudiation of church orders. That this matter is uppermost in Calvin's mind can be seen in his sermons of 1555, particularly his sermons on Deut. xviii. 15. "The Lord your God will raise up for you a prophet like me from among you, from your brethren —him you shall hear." It is interesting to observe that while later orthodoxy constantly uses this passage as a proof-text for the prophetic office of Christ, Calvin sees in it rather a guarantee for the continuing order of the ministry. "Let us note," he says, "that when Moses said that God will raise up a prophet, he was speaking of a continuing order that God wished to establish in His church, which will last until the end of time."[1] While we must wait until the following chapter to examine Calvin's exegesis of the prophetic role more fully, we may see here a clue to the development of Calvin's doctrine. The ministerial order, which is essentially prophetic, is not dependent upon ecclesiastical tradition; rather, it is founded upon the Word of God—both the Word made flesh and the written word. Christ's priestly and kingly dignity is His alone—and He has graciously chosen to share that dignity with all believers. Thus no priesthood can ever claim these powers for itself. Whenever Calvin interprets the "power of the keys," he never forgets to insist:

"Let us remember that this power (which in the Scripture is attributed to pastors) is wholly contained in and limited to the ministry of the word. For Christ has not given this power properly to these

---

[1] Second sermon on Deut. xviii, in *C. O.* 27, p. 499.

men but to His word, of which He has made these men ministers."[1]

This emphasis is consistently maintained and expanded in the last edition of the *Institutes*:

> "For these things, the remission of sins, the promise of eternal life, and the message of salvation, cannot be in the power of man.... The Word of the gospel, by whomsoever it may happen to be preached, is the very sentence of God Himself, promulgated from His heavenly tribunal, recorded in the book of life, ratified, confirmed, and fixed in heaven. Thus we see, that the power of the keys, in these passages, is no other than the preaching of the gospel, and that, considered with regard to men, it is not so much authoritative as ministerial; for, strictly speaking, Christ has not given this power to men, but to His word, of which He has appointed men to be the ministers."[2]

It is not surprising, therefore, that Calvin should stress the teaching and preaching function of the ministry of biblical times. The priest of the Old Testament was the interpreter of the law and the messenger of the word.

> "This was the covenant which God anciently made with the Levitical priests, that they should

---
[1] *Instruction in Faith*, p. 73.
[2] *Inst.*, IV.11.1 (II, p. 486).

48 DOCTRINE OF THE WORK OF CHRIST

teach their people from His mouth; He always required the same of the prophets. . . ."[1]

The prophet, accordingly, only serves to add greater clarity to the teaching of the law. God published no "new oracles" by them to be added to the law—rather they proceed from the law and merely interpret the law.[2] Thus, with reference to the power of the keys, priest and prophet in the Old Testament are analagous to pastor and teacher in the New Testament and to the ministry of the present Church:

"It is necessary to remember, that whatever authority and dignity is attributed by the Holy Spirit, in the Scripture, either to the priests and prophets under the law, or to the apostles and their successors, it is all given, not in a strict sense to the persons themselves, but to the ministry over which they were appointed, or, to speak more correctly, to the word, the ministration of which was committed to them."[3]

Since it is the Word of God that validates any ministry, Calvin could write to the Church in Frankfurt to assure that congregation that its minister, Poulain, was properly a pastor even though the formalities of the laying on of hands had been omitted.[4] For Calvin the credentials of the ministry are a proper call and fidelity

[1] *Inst.*, IV.9.2 (II, p. 435). The case of the Old Testament high priest is somewhat different. He was peculiar to Israel and there is no reason to extend either a pontiff or central church (Jerusalem) to the whole world. Moreover, says Calvin, "every one knows that the Jewish high-priest was a type of Christ." *Inst.* IV.6.2 (II, p. 369).
[2] *Inst.*, IV.8.6 (II, pp. 420, 421).   [3] *Inst.*, IV.8.2 (II, p. 417).
[4] Cf. *Letters*, ed. Bonnet, vol. 3, pp. 241 f. (December 22nd, 1555).

to the Word of God, apart from which no ceremony of ordination is efficacious. It is well known, of course, that there is no record of Calvin himself being ordained by the laying on of hands.[1] One should add, however, that Calvin does not disparage the formalities of church order. He says:

> "Now, though there is no express precept for the imposition of hands, yet since we find it to have been constantly used by the apostles, such a punctual observance of it by them ought to have the force of a precept with us. And certainly this ceremony is highly useful both to recommend to the people the dignity of the ministry, and to admonish the person ordained that he is no longer his own master, but devoted to the service of God and the Church."[2]

This stress on the "dignity of the ministry" leads to the other side of Calvin's understanding of church order. We have seen that over against the Roman claims for a special priesthood, Calvin emphasises that Christ alone is High Priest, and that Christ gives Himself so graciously that His people become a "kingdom of priests." This insight colours all that he has to say about the ministry of priest and prophet in the Old Testament, and of pastor and teacher in the New. However, Anabaptist sectaries posed an opposite peril to the church—so to stress the priesthood of all believers that the dignity of the ministry itself was lost. This extreme is of equal concern to Calvin. Satan is always

[1] Mitchell Hunter, *Teaching of Calvin*, p. 202. Cf. Doumergue, vol. 2, pp. 407 f.
[2] *Inst.*, IV.3.16 (II, p. 331).

trying to undermine the Church. In other ages he worked by causing the preaching of the pure gospel to disappear, and "in the present day he is labouring with the same malignity to overturn the ministry."[1] Let us remember that the apostolic and pastoral office is more essential to the preservation of the Church than is the light and heat of the sun or meat and drink to the nourishment of the body.[2] Let us remember Christ's word that "He that heareth you, heareth me." Calvin insists that "those who despise this discipline and this order do injury not only to men, but to God."[3] Yet with full appreciation of the dignity of the ministerial order, let us recall Paul's insistence that the Church is founded "not upon the opinions of men, not upon the priesthood, but upon the 'doctrine of the apostles and prophets.' "[4] While he does not say so, it is more than likely that Calvin's suggestion of the three offices of Christ reflects his concern for a sound basis for ministerial order, as he suggests in Chapter 15 of Book II.

It does not follow, however, that this gives exegetical justification for the triple formula. If Calvin seeks to base the prophetic role of the ministry on the prophetic office of Christ, he is in fact denying what is the essential meaning of these offices—namely, that Christ gives Himself to *all* believers. He is king and priest that His people may be "kings and priests unto God." If the prophetic office is to be given a separate status then it too must be communicated to all believers. (In this sense the prophetic office would fulfil the wish of Moses, "would God that all the Lord's peoples were

---

[1] *Inst.*, IV.1.10 (II, p. 283).   [2] *Inst.*, IV.3.2 (II, p. 319).
[3] *Instruction in Faith*, p. 72.   [4] *Inst.*, IV.2.4 (II, p. 308).

prophets and that the Lord would put His spirit upon them!" (Num. xi. 29). If, on the other hand, the prophetic office is the foundation of the ministry, it is fair to ask whether this is not in principle to do the very thing which Calvin so vigorously and rightly condemns when he considers the priestly and kingly offices. To this extent I believe that Ritschl's contention is warranted that the three offices represents a change for the worse because the practical bearing of the offices in the transference of these attributes to all believers tends to disappear.[1]

(b) *The Place of the Formula in Calvin's Thought*

However, more important than the manner in which Calvin may come to the formula is the use he himself makes of it. We need to ask ourselves whether the formula represents a peripheral or an essential theological change. We need to ask whether the formula of the three offices really fits into the structure of Calvin's thought. The usual answer has been affirmative, largely because the schema becomes a central category in later orthodoxy. I would contend that the change is peripheral rather than essential. I would go further. While Calvin suggests the formula as a theological category in his later dogmatics, he himself does no more with it —for the very good reason that he cannot make use of it. The essential structure of his doctrine of Christ's work remains two-fold. If such be the case, then the *munus triplex* is not the truest expression of his theology.

It is well to guard against overstatement. The centrality of a concept does not depend upon arithmetical

[1] Ritschl, *op. cit.*, vol. 3, p. 419.

number. In itself it does not prove anything that Calvin should have devoted only one short chapter to the three offices in his last edition of the *Institutes*, and then should make no further reference to the formula. After all, he usually speaks of the mediatorial office in the singular since the work of Christ is a unitary work. "*Officium Christi est, recta nos ad patrem manu ducere.*"[1] Christ has but one purpose in his coming—to bring us to God. Accordingly, it is not surprising that Calvin should follow the chapter on the three offices with a longer chapter entitled, "Christ's execution of the office of a Redeemer to procure our salvation." Calvin would never have had patience with the over-refinements of some of his followers who sought so to analyse the various offices that the work of Christ becomes "departmentalised"—and depersonalised. Against such temptations Calvin was guarded by his biblical realism. Emmen[2] is quite right in suggesting that Calvin felt no need of developing a more systematic exposition of the offices because for him their paradoxical unity is guaranteed by the paradoxical union of the two natures in Christ that no rationalism can ever put asunder. The work of Christ is a personal work; therefore it must be a unitary work. *Officium Christi est, recta nos ad patrem manu ducere.*

None the less, while we must remember that Calvin sees the work of the Redeemer as a unitary work, one can distinguish its inherent aspects—the messianic offices. If the formula of the three offices represents an essential emphasis in Calvin's theology it will inhere

[1] "De Scandalis quibus hodie plerique absterrentur nonnulli etiam alienantur a pura evangelii doctrina," in *C. O*: 8, p. 10.
[2] *Op. cit.*, p. 51.

THE OFFICES OF CHRIST 53

in the structure of his thought. But it does not. Whenever the office of the Redeemer appears it continues to be characterised by a two-fold character—regal and priestly.

Let us examine the last edition of the *Institutes*. In Book II, chapter 6, Calvin deals briefly with the whole sweep of Old Testament promise to show that the redemption for lost man has always been found in Christ alone, since "God never showed himself propitious to His ancient people, nor afforded them any hope of His favour, without a mediator."[1] Thus the streams of Old Testament promise become luminous in Christ "whose office it is to collect what had been scattered abroad."[2] Now what are these streams of promise? Calvin suggests that they are included in the oracles of Hannah: "The Lord shall give strength unto His *king*, and exalt the horn of His anointed," and "I will raise me up a faithful *priest*, and He shall walk before mine anointed."[3] In the remainder of the chapter Calvin develops the messianic promise with special reference to the kingly aspect.

In the following chapter the two-fold character becomes evident again in his description of the purpose

[1] *Inst.*, II.6.2 (I, p. 369).   [2] *Ibid.*

[3] *Ibid.* (I, p. 370). Italics mine. In his homily on 1 Sam. ii. 10, Calvin dwells almost exclusively upon the kingly promise, including Christ's teaching under His rule: "Especially does Hannah think of kings and the anointed of Jehovah, certainly not as though our Lord Jesus Christ reigns above God Himself, but because He has the living image of God; nor as though God rules above Christ, but because He has appointed Him judge of the world, and God Himself is the Father of our Lord Jesus Christ. Thus it is as if she said king and prophet of God, because He received from God dominion and the authority to rule. We are taught by these words that our Lord Jesus Christ was not sent by man but by God the Father who so loved the world that He did not spare His own son." Homilia 7, in *C. O.* 29, p. 314.

of Israel's adoption. Israel was to be a kingdom of priests, reflecting the heritage lost in Adam and regained in Christ, for believers are "all invested with sacerdotal and regal honours, that in a dependence on their Mediator they may venture to come boldly into the presence of God."[1] Thus the messianic promise has a two-fold character: "It must be remarked, by the way, that the kingdom, which at length was erected in the family of David, is a part of the law, and comprised under the ministry of Moses; whence it follows, that both in the posterity of David, and in the whole Levitical tribe, *as in a two-fold mirror*, Christ was exhibited to His ancient people."[2]

All this will find its ultimate expression in the cross. "Wherefore, in what is called the Apostles' Creed, there is very properly an immediate transition from the birth of Christ to His death and resurrection, in which the sum of perfect salvation consists."[3] Accordingly, in the very important chapter dealing with the cross, the kingly and priestly aspects are strongly emphasised. We need not develop here Calvin's emphasis upon the priestly character of the cross, since this is familiar enough. It should be emphasised, however, that the cross has for Calvin also a regal character. "It is not without reason," he says, "that Paul magnificently proclaims the triumph which Christ gained for Himself on the cross; as though the cross, which was full of ignominy, had been converted into a *triumphal chariot*."[4] This metaphor of the triumphal chariot, drawn from Col. ii. 15, is one of Calvin's favourite expressions and

[1] *Inst.*, II.7.1 (I, p. 378). [2] *Inst.*, II.7.2 (I, p. 378). Italics mine.
[3] *Inst.*, II.16.5 (I, p. 556). [4] *Inst.*, II.16.6 (I, p. 560). Italics mine.

constantly recurs in his exegetical writings. Thus the cross is not only the sacrifice of Christ. It is also His regal triumph over the enemy, and it becomes therefore the assurance of our own conquest in Him.[1]

If we pass from the *Institutes* to Calvin's other doctrinal writings, we can observe the same prominence of the kingly and priestly work of Christ. When he drew the Genevan reply to the Stancarian error, Calvin naturally speaks of the mediatorial office in the singular because the substance of his argument is to show that Christ is mediator in both his natures. None the less, his treatment suggests again the two-fold aspect of this one saving work.[2]

However, the most conclusive evidence is found in the *Consensus with Zurich*, regarding the Lord's Supper. The

---

[1] *Inst.*, II.16.7 (I, p. 561): "He surrendered himself to death to be, as it were, overcome by it, not that He might be absorbed in its abysses, but rather that He might destroy that, by which we should have been at length devoured; He surrendered Himself to death to be subdued, not that He might be overwhelmed by its power, but rather that He might overthrow that which threatened us, which indeed had already overcome us, and was triumphing over us. Lastly, He died 'that he might destroy him that had the power of death, that is, the devil; and deliver them who through fear of death were all their lifetime subject to bondage.' "

[2] *Responsum ad Fratres Polonos quomodo mediator sit Christus, ad refutandum stancari errorem* (1560), in *C. O.* 9, p. 339. "With reference to this matter, as the apostle argues, it was fitting that Christ, in order that He might be our brother, should partake of the nature of our flesh and blood. So in turn must we conclude that He was endowed with the same divinity as the Father in order that He might lead and direct us to the Father. This is peculiarly fitting for one who holds the office of mediator.... This is likewise applicable to the priesthood. He could not discharge this office without entering the sanctuary of heaven.... By this He clearly demonstrates that no one is fit and suitable for this office unless He partakes of the divine nature.... And it is for this reason that He is designated as priest for all time, not simply because He was chosen from men but because by the decree of the Father He took on human form to expiate sins.... And yet the prophet [i.e. David] connects these two concepts with each other: that He was made Lord and king to sit on the right hand of the Father, and that as a priest He was put in charge of the church."

Consensus dates from 1549 (with Calvin's explanatory notes added in 1554), considerably after the time when Calvin had added the triple formula to the *Institutes*. It is well to note that this tract represents Calvin's most careful and studied theological effort in order to secure unity among the reformed churches. Here again we find a clear statement of the two offices of the Redeemer. The second article states that a true knowledge of the sacraments depends upon a true knowledge of Christ, "to what end He was given us by the Father, and what blessings He has conferred upon us." This is always basic for Calvin, for Christology is always the measure of an adequate ecclesiology and doctrine of sacraments. Article IV of the *Consensus* is entitled, "Christ a Priest and King." Calvin writes:

> "Thus Christ in his fleshly form must be regarded by us as a priest who has expiated our sins by the singular sacrifice involved in His death, who by His obedience has wiped out all our iniquities; who has procured complete justice for us; who now intercedes for us, so that there is available for us an approach to the Father. He is, as it were, to be regarded as a sacrificial victim who is an atoning priest by whom God has been appeased towards the world. He is to be regarded as a brother who has transformed us from the wretched sons of Adam into the blessed sons of God. He is to be regarded as the restorer, who by the virtue of His own spirit, amends whatever is corrupt in us, that we may cease to live to the world and the flesh, and that God Himself may live in us. He is to be regarded as a king who

THE OFFICES OF CHRIST 57

enriches us with every type of blessing; who guides us and protects us with His own virtue; who equips us with spiritual weapons in order that we may stand unconquered against the devil and the world; who frees us from all harm; who guides and rules us with the sceptre of His mouth. And He must thus be regarded, that He may bring us to the true God Himself and to the Father until that is fulfilled which at length will come to pass, viz., that God is all in all."[1]

It seems evident that this passage is of considerable importance, because few writings have received such careful and loving attention. It represents Calvin's most ecumenical effort in theology.

All this is not to suggest that Calvin's doctrinal thought forgets or minimises the importance of the teaching of Christ. Calvin reminds the reader that "because Christ performs the office of a Teacher, in a station of inferiority, He ascribes the name of God to the Father, not to destroy His own Deity, but by degrees to raise us to the knowledge of it."[2] It is scarcely necessary to compile further examples of so obvious a truth. Christ is our Teacher, sent by the Father to reveal His Will.[3] He is the Light of the World, the Sun of Righteousness who dispels every cloud and who illuminates the whole world.[4]

[1] *Consensio mutua in re sacramentaria ministrorum tigurinae ecclasiae et D. Ioannis Calvini Ministri Genevensis Ecclesiae*, 1549, in C. O. 7, p. 736. I quote from the Latin because the translation in *Tracts of Reformation* omits some phrases of the original.

[2] *Inst.*, I.13.24 (I, p. 170).

[3] Cf. *Du Nom de Dieu et de son invocation*, in C. O. 10, p. 154: "For Jesus Christ, in coming into the world, was ordained by the Father our teacher and master to proclaim to us all the truth."

[4] "Sun of Righteousness" is one of Calvin's favourite descriptions for Christ. We shall consider it when we approach his commentaries.

The real question, however, is whether this revelatory aspect of Christ's mission is for Calvin best understood in terms of a formula of offices which would place it alongside the kingly and priestly offices. This is precisely what later theology does, but apparently Calvin does not do this. If we read carefully, we find that the revelatory character of Christ's work does not receive a separate messianic or "typical" treatment—rather, it belongs to His *de persona*, it permeates His kingly and priestly work. We have already seen how the *Institutes* sees two great streams of messianic promise in the Old Testament. Calvin suggests that the kingdom is essentially part of the law, and thus is already comprehended under the ministry of Moses. Accordingly, Moses is seen not as typifying a separate messianic unction, but rather as the lawgiver who anticipates the Davidic type.[1]

Because the messianic work is a redemptive work, it is in Calvin's doctrine of the Cross that we can expect to find his clearest expression of the messianic office. He constantly sees the Cross as a kingly conquest and a priestly sacrifice. Nowhere does he relate the prophetic office to the Cross. Indeed, it seems that Calvin sees a peril in trying to do so—for an exemplary theory of atonement takes from the Cross its objective and saving character.[2]

[1] Cf. above, page 54.
[2] E.g., *Contre la Secte phantastique et furieuse des Libertins qui se nomment Spirituelz* (1545), in *C. O.* 7, p. 199. Calvin sharply criticises their view of Christ as Exemplar: "When they say that Jesus Christ has abolished sin, they mean only that Jesus Christ exhibited this abolition in His own person. When they say that death was vanquished, it is only because Jesus Christ on the cross played the part of one who endured it. In His resurrection He showed Himself a victorious captain. Besides, according to their phantasy, we are all Christs."

THE OFFICES OF CHRIST 59

To sum up: In spite of the fact that Calvin suggests the formula of the three offices in the later editions of his *Institutes* and *Catechism*, he does not himself make any real use of the formula. This is certainly a curious fact which calls for further explanation. Calvin's dogmatic writings pose the problem, but his exegetical works will resolve it.[1] Christ is found in the scriptures, so to the scriptures we must go. Calvin the exegete must here explain and interpret Calvin the dogmatician. "Less than any man of his generation, or for many generations after, did he attempt to force the rigid formulas of a dogmatic system on the free and living thought of the Bible."[2] It is in his day by day expositions of the Word of God that we can expect to find those underlying motifs that govern his systematic theology.[3]

[1] Cremer makes a similar suggestion, though only in passing. He suggests that Calvin never tried to show a vital relation between the three offices of Christ in the *Institutes* because he was content only to demonstrate how we, condemned, dead and lost in ourselves, must find in Christ our redemption, life and salvation. "Thus for Calvin faith in Christ as in our High Priest and our King becomes a believing appropriation of the sacred doctrine taught of Him in the Scriptures through the Holy Spirit." *De Heilige Schrift bij Calvijn* (Utrecht, 1926), p. 49.

[2] H. R. Mackintosh, "John Calvin: Expositor and Dogmatist," in *The Review and the Expositor*, April, 1910.

[3] His biographer, Beza, estimates that Calvin preached 286 times annually, and lectured 180 times.

CHAPTER THREE

THE EXEGETICAL BASIS OF CALVIN'S DOCTRINE OF THE OFFICES OF CHRIST

IT is well to make a few preliminary remarks concerning Calvin's commentaries. By and large, the New Testament commentaries are first, beginning with his *Romans* in 1539, while Calvin was in Strasbourg. His very last commentaries are on the Old Testament, *Joshua* (1563) being the last that he himself wrote. The commentaries on the prophetical books are of two kinds. *Isaiah* was written by Calvin himself in 1550, and later revised as almost a new book. On the other hand, *Jeremiah*, *Lamentations*, the *Twelve*, *Daniel*, and lastly *Ezekiel* are in the form of lectures, taken down and edited by Bude and Joinville, sometimes but not necessarily corrected by Calvin himself.

It is thus interesting to observe that those commentaries which deal most explicitly with the content of the messianic promise are very late. (*Ezekiel*, for example, was ended abruptly at Chapter 20 by Calvin's last illness.) In his expositions of the messianic promise we would expect to find some expression of the threefold formula, and yet the fact remains that it is in these later commentaries of the prophetical books that we find instead the clearest expressions of the two-fold messianic office of Priest and King.

One can go farther. So far as I can discover, the

formula of the three offices never appears in his commentaries, and only once in his sermons, and that one instance merely in a descriptive and not in any structural manner.[1] The preceding chapter pointed to the curious fact that Calvin never made any real use of the formula in his doctrinal writings. We can see now that he did not arrive at the formula through exegesis. I do not mean to suggest, of course, that there are not numerous passages in his commentaries and sermons that speak of Christ as a prophet and teacher. I mean rather that nowhere does Calvin make this teaching a separate messianic dignity alongside with the messianic offices of king and priest. A good example is Calvin's exposition of the Cleansing of the Temple. Apparently distinguishing the Johannine account as a separate incident, he comments:

"Christ reckoned it enough to administer twice an open reproof of the profanation of it. Accordingly, when He made Himself known as a Teacher and Prophet sent by God, He took upon Himself the office of purifying the temple, in order to arouse the Jews, and make them more attentive; and this first narrative is given by John only in the second chapter of his Gospel. But now, towards the end of His course, claiming again for Himself the same power, He warns the Jews of the pollutions of the temple,

[1] The passage in question is from a sermon on Luke i. 1-4: "Our faith never looks at things in general, but always looks at God that it may have him for a Father: and it sees Him in the person of our Lord Jesus, that we may have Him for our King who governs us and has us in His protection; and then, that he may cleanse and purify us and render us acceptable to His Father God; and as Prophet, that we may be instructed of Him." *C. O.* 46, p. 6.

and at the same time points out that a new restoration is at hand.

And yet there is no reason to doubt that He declared himself to be both King and High Priest, who presided over the temple and the worship of God. This ought to be observed, lest any private individual should think himself entitled to act in the same manner."[1]

Why this is so we must now undertake to discover by considering Calvin's exegetical principles as these relate to the office of the Redeemer.

(a) *Christ in all of the Scriptures*
(1) *Calvin's principles of interpretation.*

It is not necessary here to develop in detail Calvin's doctrine of the word of God, nor his ability as an exegete, since there are useful monographs to guide the reader.[2] It is sufficient here to indicate three characteristic emphases of his exegetical method.

First is Calvin's faithfulness to the grammatico-historical method. To this he brought a wide erudition both linguistic and historical, and a passion to make clear what the Bible actually says. With all his evident messianic interest in the Old Testament, for example, Calvin ever seeks to find the historical context. For

[1] Comm. Matt. xxi. 10.
[2] The most satisfactory treatment is by Cremer, *De Heilige Schrift bij Calvijn*. Useful also is Clavier, *Etudes sur le Calvinisme* ("Calvin commentateur biblique"), Paris, 1936. Dowey includes a stimulating discussion of Calvin's view of scripture in his *Knowledge of God in Calvin's Theology*, (N.Y., Columbia U., 1952) though I believe he exaggerates the tension between Calvin's dynamic view of the Word and his view of inerrancy. The best treatment of Calvin's preaching is T. H. Parker, *The Oracles of God*. [Cf. also Biesterveld, *Calvijn als Bedienaar des Woords* (Kampen, 1897), and Nixon, *John Calvin Expository Preacher* (Grand Rapids, Wm. Eerdmans Co., 1950).]

example, of Psalm lxxii he says, "They who will have this to be simply a prediction of the Kingdom of Christ seem to twist the words very violently. And besides, we should always take care not to give the Jews good reason for reproaching us, as if we were determined by mere force of sophistry to apply to Christ what does not directly refer to Him." It is this concern which interprets both his reverence for the authority of the scriptures[1] and his freedom in textual and historical criticism as seen in his remarks on the second half of Isaiah, or 2 Peter, etc. Throughout, it is always his aim to understand the context and so to grasp the living unity of the Bible.

A second characteristic might be called Calvin's "sense of wholeness." Recognizing the organic unity of the biblical revelation, Calvin always sees the part in relation to the whole. Perhaps better than anyone in his day, and better than many since, he realised that scripture is its own best interpreter. That is precisely why a theory of inspiration is only of secondary interest to him, for his concern is the living reality of revelation.[2] In this respect his commentaries retain a vigour that many of his followers lost through such a

[1] Cf. Dowey, *Knowledge of God in Calvin's Theology*, for a fuller discussion of Calvin's doctrine of scripture. He shows that for Calvin the "how" of inspiration is a matter of subordinate interest (p. 89). However, Dowey would caution against concluding too much from this, for he sees a basic conflict between Calvin the humanist scholar and Calvin the theologian. He adduces some very interesting examples where Calvin's "lower" criticism of text does not affect his claim that the biblical writers are the "amanuenses of the Holy Spirit", concluding that Calvin reveals here an incomplete assimilation of traditional doctrine with the new manner of approaching the text. Cf. pp. 90-131.

[2] Here Georgia Harkness quite misunderstands Calvin when she concludes her discussion of Calvin's view of the Bible by saying, "But he was a thorough-going Fundamentalist." *John Calvin, the Man and His Ethic* (N. Y., Henry Holt, 1931), p. 67.

rigid view of inspiration that the Bible was reduced to a collection of scattered proof-texts to support a dogmatic system. That Calvin does not subordinate exegesis to a system will be apparent in the following pages. It is his sense of wholeness that has given his commentaries their lasting value even when the textual and critical details have become superseded. What George Adam Smith said of Calvin's commentary on Isaiah may be said of his commentaries as a whole: "To begin with, there was Calvin, and there is Calvin—still as valuable as ever for his strong spiritual power, his sanity, his moderation, his sensitiveness to the changes of the prophet's meaning."[1]

While these two qualities of his exegesis have won general approval, a third characteristic bears more directly on our subject. It is his "Christological interpretation" of the Old Testament.[2] While avoiding the excesses of some contemporary exponents of Christological interpretation, such as Wilhelm Vischer,[3] Calvin, like Luther, never forgot that the whole Bible is the manger in which Christ is found. It will help us to consider what he means by the "typical" character of the Old Testament.

Since there is one God who has made a single covenant of grace through the one mediator, Christ is present in the Old Testament as He is in the New. The

[1] G. A. Smith, *Book of Isaiah*, Intro. to vol. 2 (1890, rev. 1927, pub. Harpers, N. Y.), p. xvii.

[2] The phrase means to express Calvin's typological or spiritual interpretation of the Old Testament as a foreshadowing of Christ.

[3] W. Vischer, *The Witness of the Old Testament to Christ*, trans. A. B. Crabtree, vol. 1 (Lutterworth, London, 1949). Note what Vischer can do with the "red heifer" of Num. xix. 2. Yet Hebert, *Throne of David*, and Phythian Adams, *Fulness of Israel*, are good examples of a return to "Christological interpretation" without sacrificing critical principles.

institutions and history of Israel are sacramental signposts pointing beyond themselves to their fulfilment in Christ. Messianic promise, therefore, is not confined to a number of explicit predictions, but rather is rooted in the whole texture of the Old Testament. Calvin had a clear sense of the difference between allegory and type.

Allegory is the representation by a figurative story of something metaphorically suggested but not stated. One need not enlarge upon the extravagances to which the allegorical method is subject. No less than Luther, Calvin rejects such exegesis vigorously. "I have elsewhere reminded you, that we are to avoid those futile refinements which of themselves vanish away. Allegories, I know, delight many; but we ought reverently and soberly to interpret the prophetic writings, and not to fly in the clouds, but ever to fix our foot on solid ground."[1]

On the other hand, a type is an institution, act, or person, appointed by God to prefigure effectively some aspects of the redemption accomplished by Christ. As a type ($\tau\acute{u}\pi os$), it bears a stamp put upon it by God, a meaning accordingly which is essential to it. Type and allegory differ in three important respects. The subject of an allegory is a mere historical event occurring in the ordinary course of things, while a type is expressly appointed to teach some appointed truth. Again, the allegorical sense is a fictitious meaning put upon a narrative for the sake of didactic use, while the explanation of a type is inherent in its essential meaning. Finally, allegory may be used in a very wide variety, while a type must relate directly to the one redemptive

[1] Comm. Zech. vi. 1-3. On this basis Calvin will vigorously deny the allegorical interpretation of the prodigal son, the "Lucifer" passage of Isa. xiv. etc.

purpose of God. In the use of typology, the New Testament must be our guide.

For Calvin, such a "typical" reading of the Old Testament constitutes a necessary exegetical approach, since it is based on the unity of God's redemptive purpose. Messianic promise ought not to be limited to certain direct predictions, for it is rooted in all of Old Testament history and institutions—supremely in the kingdom and priesthood. Calvin knows, of course, how easily type can slide into allegory. When speaking of Hezekiah as a type of Christ, he says, "Let no man imagine that I am here pursuing allegories, to which I am averse, and that this is the reason why I do not interpret the passage as relating directly to Christ; but, because in Christ alone is found the stability of that frail kingdom, the likeness which Hezekiah bore leads us to Christ, as it were, by the hand. I am, therefore, disposed to view Hezekiah as a figure [i.e. type] of Christ, that we may learn how great will be His beauty."[1] Where the difference between type and allegory is not immediately apparent, Calvin would say, we must let the New Testament be our guide. For example, Jonah was not a type of Christ because he was sent to the Gentiles, but because he returned to life again.[2] Or again, Calvin holds that Matthew rightly interprets Hos. xi. 1 Christologically, not because it is a definite prediction, but because "Christ cannot be separated from his Church, as the body will be mutilated and imperfect without a head. Whatever then happened formerly in the Church, ought at length to be fulfilled by the head."[3]

[1] Comm. Isa. xxxiii. 17.   [2] Comm. Jonah i. 1, 2.
[3] Comm. Hos. xi. 1.

It is well to make a further distinction between type and comparison (illustration). In a comparison, an historical event, whether natural or by the special intervention of God, is used by a later writer or speaker to illustrate, by comparison, some fact or doctrine he may be treating. On the other hand, in a type the meaning it prefigures is meant for those among whom the type is set up. Calvin is careful to observe this distinction. Jacob's ladder, he says, is a "similitude" rather than a type.[1]

From these preliminary observations we pass now to the interpretation itself. Christ is present in all of the Scriptures, for "God never showed Himself propitious to His ancient people, nor afforded them any hope of His favour, without a Mediator."[2]

(2) *The Relationship of Old Testament to New: Law and Gospel.*

When Calvin discusses the Old Testament's relationship to the New in the *Institutes*,[3] he stresses first their similarity, since God has made a single covenant with His people. This covenant may vary in its administration, but is substantially one in its gracious content. Both Old and New Testaments have the same three promises: eternal life, a covenant based on unmerited grace, and a knowledge and possession of Christ as the Mediator. Although the promises are the same, however, their administration is quite different, for the New

[1] Comm. Gen. xxviii. 12. In developing the similitude, Calvin writes: "It is Christ alone, therefore, who connects heaven and earth: He is the only Mediator, who reaches from heaven down to earth: He is the medium through which the fulness of all celestial blessings flows down to us, and through whom we, in turn, ascend to God."

[2] *Inst.*, II.6.2 (I, p. 369).   [3] *Inst.*, II, chapters 10 and 11.

Testament leaves the shadows and figures of the Old for the direct contemplation of God's grace through the gospel. There is the difference between law and gospel.

One should observe that Calvin does not place law and gospel in such sharp antithesis as does Luther. For Calvin the law has three parts: it contains the doctrine of life, it contains threatenings and promises, and it contains the covenant of grace which, being founded on Christ, contains within itself all the special promises.[1] It is therefore not correct to say that law is meritorious while gospel is gracious, for the law also is gracious since it embraces Christ. "Let us therefore learn to maintain inviolable this sacred tie between law and gospel, which many improperly attempt to break."[2] The law therefore includes the gospel. "Without Christ there is in the law nothing but inexorable rigour, which adjudges all mankind to the wrath and curse of God . . . but David, in praising it as he here does, speaks of the whole doctrine of the law, which includes also the gospel, and, therefore, under the law he comprehends Christ."[3] Yet law remains distinct from gospel since the administration of the law is so different from that of the gospel.[4] The law condemns us by its demands—and

[1] Cf. the preface to Calvin's commentary on Isaiah.
[2] Comm. Matt. v. 17. Cf. also Comm. 2 Cor. iv. 3: "When Christ is included in the law, the sun shines forth through the midst of the clouds, so that men have light enough for their use; but when Christ is disjoined from it, there is nothing left but darkness, or a false appearing of light, that dazzles men's eyes, instead of assisting them."
[3] Comm. Ps. xix. 8.
[4] Comm. Hab. ii. 4. "The law agrees with the gospel, indeed it includes it, but though there is complete accord, the law does not accord with the gospel in regard to justification, 'any more than light with darkness,' for the law promises life to those who serve God; and the promise is conditional, dependent on the merit of works. The gospel also does indeed promise righteousness under condition; but it has no respect to the merit of works. . . ."

so leads us to Christ. The gospel gives life by presenting Christ to us visibly. "For what is proposed to us in Christ, unless what God had promised in the law, and therefore Christ is called the end of the law, and elsewhere its spirit, for if the law be separated from Christ, it is like a dead letter: Christ alone gives it life."[1] The law is then abrogated for the Christian in the sense that it is no longer the instrument of death. It has been transformed into an instrument of life.

But Christ is not only the "end of the law." He is also the "end of the prophets."[2] What is Old Testament prophecy?

To understand the role of the prophets, says Calvin, we must relate them to the law "from which they derived their doctrine, like streams from a fountain."[3] Since their prophecies are expositions of the three-fold content of the law, they are "*appendages* of the law, and are all briefly summed up in the law."[4] Calvin's description, "*appendages*," is significant. "It must yet be observed, that the prophetic office was not separated from the law, for all the prophecies which followed the law were, as it were, its *appendages*: so that they included nothing new, but were given that the people might be more fully retained in their obedience to the law."[5]

[1] Comm. Ezek. xvi. 61.
[2] The phrase, "Christ the end of the law and the prophets" is recurrent in Calvin's writing.
[3] Preface to Comm. on Isaiah.   [4] *Ibid.* Italics mine.
[5] Comm. Mal. iv. 4. Cf. also Comm. Acts vii. 37: "Stephen endeavours undoubtedly to prove by these words that Christ is the end of the law; although he does not express the same in plain words. . . . The prophets were, indeed, interpreters of the law, and all their doctrine was, as it were, an addition or *appendage* to those things which were uttered by Moses. . . ." Italics mine.

The prophetic office was accordingly "an extraordinary office, when God took others as the ministers of His word besides the priests."[1] Teaching is a sacerdotal function in the Old Testament, but God meant to condemn the priests by transferring their work to others.[2] It follows, then, that to say that Christ is the end of the prophets is not really different from saying that He is the end of the law. And so, when Christ appeared, "we arrive at the close of prophetic times, and hence His advent is called the fulness of times."[3]

Since Christ is the eternal Mediator, apart from whom God never has been known, it is not surprising that Calvin should see Christ not only in the types and promises of the Old Testament, but also in its theophanies. The mysterious Angel of the Lord who received the title of Jehovah was "undoubtedly the only-begotten Son of God . . . I willingly receive what ancient writers teach on the subject—that when Christ anciently appeared in human form, it was a prelude to the mystery which was afterwards exhibited when God was manifested in the flesh."[4] For Calvin this exposition is simply a corollary of his principle that because God's purpose is one, there has always been the one Mediator—typified in the law, revealed in the gospel, active before Bethlehem as He has been active since Easter. "We must draw from the fulness of Christ

[1] Comm. Zech. vii. 1-3.
[2] Comm. Micah iii. 11, 12. "We have said elsewhere, that it happened through the idleness of the priests, that prophets were added to them, for prophecying belonged to them, until being content with the altar, they neglected the office of teaching."
[3] Comm. Dan. ix. 25.
[4] Comm. Josh. v. 14. Cf. also Comm. Ex. xxiii. 20.

everything good, that we desire for our salvation, because such is the determination of God—not to communicate Himself or His gifts to men, otherwise than by His Son."¹

(b) *The Office of the Redeemer*

(1) *Terminology*

Before approaching Calvin's exegesis of the redemptive work of Christ, it may be well to note how he uses the term "office." To begin with, Calvin uses *munus* and *officium* interchangeably, and occasionally *pars*. For example, ". . . we should yet be ever miserable, except we had Christ as our head, to perform the office (*officio*) of a king and of a priest. This, then, is the only true happiness of the church, even to be in subjection to Christ, so that he may exercise toward us the two offices (*munus*) described here."²

Moreover, Calvin uses the term "office" in a very free manner. "Office" may mean "position," "public office," etc. It may also mean "work," "service," or "function." For example, God "fulfils the office of a physician rather than of a judge."³ When speaking of regeneration and forgiveness, Calvin writes, "Observe

¹ Comm. Col. i. 19.
² Comm. Jer. xxxiii. 17, 18. In the later theology, *munus* acquires a more specific character than *officium*. That this is not so in Calvin can be easily seen in the following examples: (1) *on office in general*: "The cause of death is Adam, and we die in him: hence Christ whose office (*officium*) it is to restore to us what we lost in Adam, is the cause of life to us," Comm. 1 Cor. xv. 21. On the other hand, "Nor is the title 'Christ' given to Him here without reason, for it designates the office (*munus*) to which he was appointed by the Father." Comm. 1 John v. 1. (2) *on particular offices*: ". . . the royal power of Christ is combined with the office (*officio*) of priest," Comm. Gen. xiv. 18. On the other hand, "the benediction pertained especially to his sacerdotal office (*munus*)," Comm. Gen. xiv. 18.
³ Comm. Gen. iii. 19.

72 DOCTRINE OF THE WORK OF CHRIST

... that these two offices of Christ are conjoined in such a manner as to be, notwithstanding, distinguished from each other."[1] Or again, Calvin will contrast "the office of the law" to the "office of the gospel."[2]

However, while Calvin uses the word in a very free manner, it does not follow that the concept of the offices of Christ is for him a purely metaphorical or figurative expression. Calvin would vigorously dispute Ritschl's contention that the "legal" connotation of offices is inapplicable to Christ. On the contrary, Calvin always insists upon the objective and representative character of Christ's work. When used in this particular sense, "office" denotes a divine appointment and not merely an individual choice.

To sum up: Calvin's free use of the term "office" guards him against making the work of Christ impersonal or "departmentalised" by insisting upon its unitary character. Yet, at the same time, Calvin recognises the public and "official" character of Christ's work as the divine appointment of God's redemptive purpose. "For it is the office of Christ to take away sins, and for this end He was sent by the Father; and it is by faith that we partake of Christ's virtue."[3]

(c) *The Messiah*

Officium Christi est recta nos ad patrem manu ducere. From a general description of the work of Christ we pass now to a closer examination. This will involve three considerations in Calvin's exegesis: the messianic name,

[1] Comm. 1 Cor. i. 30.   [2] Comm. 2 Cor. iii. 7.
[3] Comm. 1 John iii. 5.

the messianic promise, and the New Testament fulfilment.

(1) *The Messianic Name*

Our study has already made apparent that any doctrine of Christ's work revolves around an understanding of His messianic title. "By the surname 'Christ,' Anointed, Matthew points out His office, to inform the readers that this was not a private person, but one divinely anointed to perform the office of Redeemer."[1] When the Fourth Gospel closes with the purpose, "These are written that ye might believe that Jesus is the Christ, the Son of God; and that believing ye might have life through His name," Calvin comments: "For John did not seize upon an empty and unmeaning title to adorn the Son of God, but included, under the name 'Christ,' all the offices which the prophets ascribed to Him."[2]

Now, what offices are here included? Calvin's answer is crystal clear—the messianic unction is a kingly and a priestly anointing. Let us note three representative passages dealing with the title. Commenting on the nativity passage of Luke ii. 25, Calvin writes:

> "Jesus is called the Lord's Christ, because He was anointed by the Father, and at the same time that He received the Spirit, received also the title of King and Priest."[3]

Commenting on Peter's confession of faith in Matt. xvi. 16, he writes:

[1] Comm. Matt. i. 16.   [2] Comm. John xx. 31.
[3] Comm. Luke ii. 25.

74 DOCTRINE OF THE WORK OF CHRIST

"Peter's confession is short, but it embraces all that is contained in our salvation: for the designation 'Christ' or Anointed, includes both an everlasting Kingdom and an everlasting Priesthood, to reconcile us to God, and, by expiating our sins through His sacrifice, to obtain for us a perfect righteousness, and, having received us under His protection, to uphold and supply and enrich us with every description of blessings."[1]

Finally, commenting upon Peter's words to Cornelius, affirming that "God anointed Jesus of Nazareth" (Acts x. 38):

"The metaphor of anointing is usual so often as mention is made of the gifts of the Holy Ghost. It is now applied to the person of Christ, because by this means He was consecrated a king and priest by His Father."[2]

Such examples, drawn from the commentaries of 1555 and 1560, are conclusive. It is true that in his *Institutes* and *Catechism*, since 1545, he had adopted the triple formula, relating the prophetic office also to the messianic name, since "prophets also were anointed with holy oil."[3] In this, of course, later theology followed him. Yet Calvin must have sensed that this addition lacked exegetical basis, for Elisha is the only example in the Old Testament, and his case at best is problematic.[4] Since, as we have seen, his exegesis studiously

---
[1] Comm. Matt. xvi. 16.   [2] Comm. Acts x. 38.
[3] *Inst.*, II.15.2 (I, p. 542).
[4] Cf. 1 Kings xix. Elijah is told to anoint Elisha. Yet the narrative says nothing about an anointing with oil; it only says that Elijah cast his mantle upon Elisha.

seeks to avoid reading into the biblical text what is not there, the triple formula never appears in his commentaries. Perhaps nowhere is his faithfulness as a exegete more clearly seen. It would seem that in this instance Calvin the exegete refuses to follow Calvin the systematiser.

(2) *The Messianic Promise*

Having already seen that for Calvin the messianic hope is woven into the texture of Israel's redemptive history, let us look more closely at Calvin's interpretation of Old Testament promise.

Let us recall that in the *Institutes*, Calvin suggests the general principle that in the institutions of the kingdom and priesthood "*as in a two-fold mirror*, Christ was exhibited to the view of His ancient people."[1] The structural and organic union which belongs to these two institutions constitutes the messianic promise. "Hence, whenever our salvation is treated of, let these two things be remembered, that we cannot be reckoned God's sons unless He freely expiate our sins, and thus reconcile Himself to us; and then not unless He also rule us by His Spirit. *Now we must hold, that what God hath joined, man ought not to separate.*"[2] This recurrent emphasis provides the clue to our understanding of Calvin's exposition.

It is illuminating to test this conclusion by noting the scriptural context of a number of representative passages. At the risk of a pedantic treatment, I have divided these passages under four headings: (1) where the biblical context directly suggests the double office,

[1] *Inst.*, II.7.2 (I, p. 378).   [2] Comm. Ezek. xi. 19-20. Italics mine.

(2) where the context indirectly suggests the double office, (3) where the context does not suggest it at all, and (4) where the context would lead us to expect the triple.

(1) Under the first heading, of course, belong those passages that refer to Melchizidec, and so treat of his two-fold office as embracing all of Christ's redemptive activity.

> "The sum of the whole is, that Christ would thus be the king next to God, and also that He should be anointed priest, and that forever: which it is very useful for us to know, in order that we may learn that the royal power of Christ is combined with the office of priest. The same Person, therefore, who was constituted the only and eternal Priest, in order that He might reconcile us to God and who, having made expiation, might intercede for us, is also a King of infinite power to secure our salvation, and to protect us by His guardian care. Hence it follows that, relying on His advocacy, we may stand boldly in the presence of God, who will, we are assured, be propitious to us; and that trusting in His invincible arm we may securely triumph over enemies of every kind. *But they who separate one office from the other, rend Christ asunder*, and subvert their own faith, which is deprived of half its support...."[1]

One of Calvin's sermons develops this union of the two offices still further:

[1] Comm. Gen. xiv. 18. Italics mine. Cf. also Comm. Ps. cx. 4.

"Indeed, if we separate one from the other, the faith we have in our Lord Jesus Christ would be very feeble, and would no longer have a basis either firm or sure. *For there are two things necessary for our salvation,* on the one hand that God accept us as righteous, and acknowledges us as His children; on the other hand that we may be led by His hand, that we be kept and protected by His invincible power. If we should wish to take away one of these points it would only fill half (of our need). Here is how: let us suppose that God is propitious to us and that He no longer imputes to us our sins. If, however, the devil had power over us and we were exposed as prey to all the assaults that He levelled at us, would we not still be poor lost persons? On the other hand, if God only unfurled His power for our defence and we were not reconciled to Him, and were not accounted righteous, we would still certainly have to come to an accounting. And alas for us if we should be judged without mercy. But we know that all our righteousness rests on this, that God has pity upon us, that He covers all our sins. It was necessary then that our Lord Jesus Christ appeared as King and Priest. . . ."[1]

Melchizidec's uniqueness, of course, lies in the fact that he alone combined the offices of priest and king, something forbidden in the law. "Under the law, God would have some to be kings, and others to be priests; nor was it allowable to mix up the one office with the other; but He, of whom it is said that He should be

[1] Second sermon on Melchizidec, *C. O.* 23, p. 655. Italics mine.

priest like Melchizidec, is honoured with the title of king."[1] Calvin notes that Uzziah had been smitten for presuming the priestly office.[2] On this basis Melchizidec occupies an unusual position and "bore the image of Christ."[3] Beyond this Calvin does not press the analogy lest he slide into allegory.[4]

(2) A second group includes passages where the scriptural context indirectly suggests a two-fold messianic work. For example, where the kingdom and priesthood, or Jerusalem and Zion, or throne and sanctuary are mentioned (whether successively or together), Calvin often takes the occasion to point to the two-fold character of the messianic promise. Here are a few examples:

Commenting on Ps. ii. 6 ("Yet have I set my king upon my holy hill of Zion"), Calvin writes:

"And although David in these words had a regard to the promise of God, and recalled the attention of himself and others to it, yet, at the same time, he meant to signify that his own reign is holy and inseparably connected with the temple of God. But this applies more appropriately to the Kingdom of Christ, which we know to be both spiritual and joined to the priesthood, and this is the principal part of the worship of God."[5]

---

[1] Comm. Ex. xxviii.   [2] Comm. Heb. v. 6. Also Comm. Ps. cx. 4.
[3] Comm. Gen. xiv. 18.
[4] Calvin rejects the scholastic exegesis which saw in the bread and wine offered Abraham a figure of the eucharist.
[5] Comm. Ps. ii. 6.

THE EXEGETICAL BASIS

On Ps. xx. 1, 2 ("The name of the God of Jacob defend thee; send thee help from the sanctuary, and strengthen thee out of Zion"):

> "Since Christ our King, being an everlasting priest, never ceases to make intercession with God, the whole body of the Church should unite in prayer with Him.... But as God, by appointing mount Sion to be the place where the faithful should continually worship Him, had joined the kingdom and the priesthood together, David, in putting into the lips of the people a prayer for help out of Sion, doubtless had an eye to *this sacred bond of union*."[1]

On Ps. lxxviii 69-70 ("And he built His sanctuary like high palaces, like the earth which He hath established for ever. He chose David also His servant, and took Him from the sheepfolds"):

> "After having made mention of the temple, the prophet now proceeds to speak of the kingdom; for these two things were the chief signs of God's choice of His ancient people, and of His favour towards them; and Christ also has appeared as our king and priest, to bring a full and perfect salvation to us."[2]

On Ps. cxxii. 4 ("Jerusalem . . . whither the tribes go up, the tribes of the Lord, unto the testimony of Israel, to give thanks unto the name of the Lord"):

---

[1] Comm. Ps. xx. 1, 2. Italics mine.   [2] Comm. Ps. lxxviii. 69, 70.

80   DOCTRINE OF THE WORK OF CHRIST

"*All our salvation depends upon these two points*, first, that Christ has been given to be our priest; and, secondly, that He has been established king to govern us."[1]

On Jer. xvii. 25, 26 ("Then shall there enter into the gates of this city kings and princes sitting upon the throne of David. . . . And they shall come from the cities of Judah. . . . bring burnt-offerings and sacrifices . . . unto the house of the Lord."):

"Here he mentions the second part of the blessing; for the whole people would be preserved safe in the possession of their kingdom and priesthood, as in both the favour of God appeared; for both the king and the priest were types of Christ. For as by the priesthood they knew that God was propitious to them, they being reconciled to Him by sacrifices, and as by the kingdom they knew that God was the protector and guardian of their safety, so *these two things constituted a real and complete happiness.*"[2]

On Jer. xxxiii. 17, 18 ("For thus saith the Lord: David shall never want a man to sit upon the throne of the house of Israel; neither shall the priests, the Levites, want a man before me. . . ."):

"The safety of the people, as it is well known, was secured by these two things; for without a king they were like an imperfect or a maimed body, and without a priesthood there was nothing but ruin; for the priest was, as it were, the mediator between God and

---
[1] Comm. Ps. cxxii. 4. Italics mine.
[2] Comm. Jer. xvii. 26. Italics mine.

the people, and the king represented God. . . . But this passage ought to be carefully noticed, for we hence gather, that though all other things were given to us according to our wishes, we should yet be ever miserable, except we had Christ as our head, to perform the office of a king and a priest. This, then, is the only true happiness of the Church, even to be in subjection to Christ, so that He may exercise towards us the two offices described here."[1]

With reference to Hos. viii. 4 ("They have set up kings, but not by me: they have made princes, and I knew it not; of their silver and their gold have they made idols. . . .").

"The salvation of that people, we know, was, as it were, founded on a certain kingdom and priesthood; and by these two things God testified that He was allied to the children of Abraham. We know where the happiness of the godly is deposited, even in Christ, for Christ is the fulness of a blessed life because He is a king and a priest. . . ."[2]

As we might expect, Calvin makes the same emphasis when commenting on Zech. vi. 9-11, where the priest Joshua receives the double crown.[3]

---

[1] Comm. Jer. xxxiii. 17-18.   [2] Comm. Hos. viii. 4.
[3] Comm. Zech. vi. 9-11. Calvin follows the translation "He shall be a priest upon His throne," of course, rather than the present reading of the RSV, "there shall be a priest by His throne." Calvin comments, "Here then we find a union of royalty and priesthood in the same person, which had never been the case; for God had in His law made a distinction between the two offices. . . . It is then no wonder that God brought forth the high priest Joshua, who was a type and representative of Christ, and he brought him forth with a double crown, because he who was to come would unite, according to what follows, the priesthood with the kingly office."

F

(3) There are a number of interesting passages where the double office is not suggested at all, but where Calvin deals with them notwithstanding. It becomes apparent that the two-fold character of the messianic promise is for him such a clear teaching of scripture and such a needed clue to messianic prediction that he often spontaneously enlarges upon this theme. For example, on Lam. v. 16 ("The crown is fallen from our heads: woe unto us that we have sinned.") :

> "By the crown of the head He no doubt understands all those ornaments by which that people had been adorned. They had a kingdom and priesthood, which were *like two luminaries or two precious jewels*; they had also other things by which the Lord had adorned them."[1]

On Jer. xxii. 1-3 ("O king of Judah, that sittest upon the throne of David") :

> "For it was a priestly kingdom, and a type of that celestial kingdom which was afterwards fully revealed in Christ."[2]

On Dan. ix. 25 ("Know therefore and understand, that from the going forth of the commandment to restore and to build Jerusalem unto the Messiah the Prince shall be seven weeks. . . .") :

> "Clearly enough the angel speaks of Christ, of whom both kings and priests under the law were a type and figure."[3]

[1] Comm. Lam. v. 16. Italics mine. [2] Comm. Jer. xxii. 1-3.
[3] Comm. Dan. ix. 25.

THE EXEGETICAL BASIS 83

Many other parallels could be added.

(4) Of special interest are those passages which deal with kings, priests, and prophets. Since we have already seen that Calvin invariably uses references to kings and priests to point to the two-fold character of messianic promise, certainly here, if anywhere, we might expect him to point to the triple office which he has long since added to the *Institutes*. If the triple formula is at all basic to his thinking, it will appear in such passages. But this is not the case. On the contrary, Calvin uses these very passages to point directly again to the double office of Christ—to the neglect of the prophetic office. Let us take, for example, Jer. iv. 9 ("And it shall come to pass at that day, saith the Lord, that the heart of the king shall perish, and the heart of the princes; and the priests shall be astonished, and the prophets shall wonder"). Calvin will point to the seriousness of the offence because the king prefigures Christ. But he does not go on to suggest a prefiguring of the three-fold office of Christ.[1]

Another example is Jer. xxxii. 32 ("Because of all the evil of the children of Israel and of the children of Judah, which they have done to provoke me to anger, they, their kings, their princes, their priests, and their prophets. . . ."). Calvin comments:

> "And doubtless, the kings with their counsellors ought to have been one eye, the priests and the prophets the other; for the two eyes in a true and legitimate government are the judges and pastors of the Church."[2]

[1] Comm. Jer. iv. 9.   [2] Comm. Jer. xxxii. 32.

Significantly here, he couples priests and prophets as he does kings and counsellors. That is to say, the prophetic office is not given an independent status but is here included under the sacerdotal. While the passage is not directly related to Christ, it reflects the same "Grundmotif" of Calvin's thought.

One final example will suffice. Jer. xiii. 13 reads: "Thus saith the Lord, behold, I will fill all the inhabitants of this land, even the kings that sit upōn David's throne, and the priests, and the prophets, and all the inhabitants of Jerusalem, with drunkenness." Calvin comments that such a judgment might seem unjust to them, "for we know with what high commendations God had spoken of the kingdom of David. As to the priesthood, we also know that it was a type of the priesthood of Christ. . . ."[1] Significantly, he does not go on to suggest that the prophet also is a type.

Such illustrations are conclusive. For Calvin the two-fold nature of the messianic promise forms a structural and organic union. "Now we must hold," says Calvin, "that what God hath joined, man ought not to separate."[2]

(3) *The New Testament Fulfilment*

What is true of the Old Testament promise is true also of its New Testament fulfilment. To be sure, the New Testament portrait of Christ is too rich and varied to be completely realised in any scheme, yet throughout

[1] Comm. Jer. xiii. 13. It is well to note that Jeremiah is among his latest commentaries, appearing with Lamentations in 1563.
[2] Comm. Ezek. xi. 19-20.

THE EXEGETICAL BASIS 85

Calvin's exposition the two-fold activity of the Saviour continually converges. "It was indeed an inestimable honour, that the Son of God, when about to commence His reign and priesthood, had chosen Capernaum for the seat of His *palace and sanctuary*."[1] Accordingly, while we shall deal separately with the kingly and priestly offices, it will be well to remember Calvin's principle that "what God hath joined, man ought not to separate."

(d) Christ our King

The New Testament message is the gospel of the Kingdom. Jesus does not merely herald its coming; rather, He is its coming. "The appearance of Christ and His Kingdom mean the same thing."[2] Since this is so, we need not here describe the Kingdom in general terms, but may confine ourselves to the Kingdom as Christ's reign.

Calvin would insist that Christ is lord over us as God's messianic king who rules for God and unto God.

> "We now perceive the amount of what is stated here, that the Father has given to the Son a kingdom, that He may govern heaven and earth according to His pleasure. But this might appear to be very absurd, that the Father, surrendering His right to govern, should remain unemployed in heaven, like a private person. The answer is easy. This is said both

---

[1] Comm. Matt. xi. 23. Italics mine.

[2] Comm. 2 Tim. iv. 1. The passage in question refers to the second advent, but the meaning applies equally here. It expresses what Origen called "autobasileia."

in regard to God and to men; for no change took place in the Father, when He appointed Christ to be supreme king and lord of heaven and earth; for He is the Son, and works in Him. But since, when we wish to rise to God, all our senses immediately fail, Christ is placed before our eyes as a lively image of the invisible God."[1]

Christ acts as the Father's "vice-regent in governing the world."[2] Calvin suggests that in one sense the Son already exercised His eternal dominion before the incarnation, which reign was typified in the Davidic kingdom. However, it is necessary to distinguish the eternal dominion of the Son from His reign as the incarnate redeemer.

Calvin does not attempt to fix any time in the life of Christ when He began to reign, for the kingdom comes in Him. He is king—He does not become king. Accordingly, Calvin avoids the tendency of later protestant dogmatics which confined the kingly office to the state of exaltation. On the contrary, Calvin can say that even the penitent thief "adores Christ as a King while on the gallows, celebrates His kingdom in the midst of shocking and worse than revolting abasement, and declares Him, when dying, to be the author of life."[3] And the Lord's answer shows that "though Christ had not yet made a public triumph over death, still He displays the efficacy and fruit of His death in the midst of His humiliation. And in this way He shows He never was deprived of the power of His kingdom."[4] "Now if

[1] Comm. John v. 22.
[2] Comm. John xx. 26.
[3] Comm. Luke xxii. 42.
[4] Comm. Luke xxii. 43.

THE EXEGETICAL BASIS 87

a robber, by his faith, elevated Christ, while hanging on the cross . . . to a heavenly throne, woe to our sloth if we do not behold Him with reverence while sitting at the right hand of God."[1] For the exaltation is the public manifestation of His reign. Figuratively speaking, therefore, Calvin can say that Christ began His reign at the resurrection, or at His ascension, or even at His final coming in glory.[2] It is scarcely necessary to add that, if Calvin refused to fix the date of the kingdom's origin, he is equally impatient with attempts to reduce it to a temporal realm.[3]

Christ's kingdom embraces two stages—a present and a future. It means redemption in this life, yet it also looks upon this life as a prelude to the life beyond. When Christ appeared, the kingdom was "extended far and wide, so as to occupy the whole world from one end to the other."[4] He reigns to-day, for His kingdom is "every day growing and making improvement, while at the same time perfection is not yet attained, nor will be until the final day of reckoning. Thus both things hold true—that all things are now subject to Christ,

[1] Comm. Luke xxii. 43.

[2] E.g. Comm. Gal. i. 1, "The resurrection of Christ is the commencement of His reign"; Comm. John xx. 17, "by His ascension to heaven He should enter into the possession of the kingdom which had been promised Him. . . ."; 2 Tim. iv. 1, "His kingdom will therefore be established at that time when, having vanquished His enemies, and either removed or reduced to nothing every opposing power, He shall display His majesty."

[3] E.g. Comm. Acts vii. 56, "Therefore the whole text is a metaphor. . . . I confess, indeed, that speaking properly, that is, philosophically, there is no place above the heavens. But this is sufficient for me, that it is perverse doting to place Christ anywhere save only in heaven, and above the elements of the world." Similarly we might add that Calvin has no use for chiliasm.

[4] Comm. Ps. xlvii. 8.

and that this subjection will, nevertheless, not be complete until the day of resurrection, because that which is now only begun will then be completed."[1] And always, the goal of the Kingdom is the Glory of God.[2]

(1) *Christ our Victor*

In any discussion of the reign of Christ, it is well to begin with Calvin's most recurrent theme—the regal conquest of Christ over the devil, death, and sin. Here, certainly, Calvin's commentaries and sermons confirm and strengthen the emphasis of his *Institutes*. The Cross is not only a sacrifice for sin. It is a royal victory. Mankind is under the tyranny of Satan. But a stronger has "bound the strong man" (Matt. xii. 29). "Now this kind of redemption Christ shows to be necessary, in order to wrench from the devil, by main force, what He will never quit till He is compelled. By these words He informs us, that it is vain for men to expect deliverance, till Satan has been subdued by a violent struggle."[3] Here Calvin is one with Luther in stressing the "classic" view of atonement. "By means of His crucifixion salvation was obtained for the world, and Christ Himself obtained a splendid triumph over death and Satan."[4] It was as a conqueror that Jesus entered Jerusalem for His great encounter with evil.[5] The metaphor of the Cross as a triumphal chariot, which we have seen in the *Institutes*, is a recurrent expression in

---

[1] Comm. Phil. ii. 10.   [2] Cf. Comm. 1 Cor. xv. 24.
[3] Comm. Matt. xii. 29.   [4] Comm. John vi. 15.
[5] Comm. John xii. 12, ". . . before He is dragged to the cross, He wishes to be solemnly acknowledged by the people as their king; nay, He openly declares that He commences His reign by advancing to His death."

his commentaries and sermons.[1] While later Calvinism has tended to formulate the atonement primarily in sacrificial and penal terms, Calvin himself never separated it from the kingly office. In the first place, cross and resurrection are so closely related that "the resurrection of Christ does not lead us away from the cross."[2] It is impossible to speak of one without the other. A more important reason, however, lies in Calvin's insistence that, since the cross effects the work of redemption, it must necessarily be a kingly as well as a priestly work. So it is precisely in the cross that Christ appears as our Deliverer, "God's Lieutenant,"[3] our "valiant and illustrious General."[4]

[1] E.g. Comm. Acts xvi. 22, "For seeing that those persecutions which we must suffer for the testimony of the gospel are remnants of the sufferings of Christ, like as our Prince turned the cross, which was accursed, into a *triumphal chariot*, so He shall, in like sort, adorn the prisons and gibbets of His followers, that they may there triumph over Satan and all the wicked."
Comm. Col. ii. 15, "For as He had previously compared the cross to a signal trophy or show of triumph, in which Christ led about His enemies, so He now also compares it to a *triumphal car*, in which He showed Himself conspicuously to view. . . . For there is no tribunal so distinguished, no chariot so elevated, as is the gibbet on which Christ has subdued death and the devil, the prince of death; nay more, has utterly trodden them under His feet."
First sermon on Isa. liii, "It is true that His having been raised on the gibbet was an opprobrium in the eyes of men. But the prophet mocks the devil and defies the whole world by saying that He will be truly exalted, and that when He shall have been exposed to such shame that everyone will have stuck out his tongue at Him and vomited up against Him his blasphemies and villainies, yet He is seated on His throne, as we already have proven from the passage from Saint Paul. And in the other place he said especially that the Cross, although apparently it was a gibbet full of shame, was, as it were, a triumphant chariot. . . ."
C. O. 35, p. 602. Trans. L. Nixon, *The Gospel According to Isaiah* (Grand Rapids, Wm. B. Eerdmans, 1953), p. 20.
[2] Comm. Gal. vi. 14.
[3] E.g. First Sermon on Isa. liii, "Let us not confine ourselves to His sufferings alone . . . but let us link the resurrection with the death, and know that He, having been crucified, is nevertheless seated as Lieutenant of God His Father, to exercise sovereign dominion and to have all power in heaven and on earth." C. O. 35, p. 602.
[4] Comm. Isa. liii. 12.

I believe later Calvinism has too easily confined Calvin's doctrine of atonement to Anselmic terms. "No language, indeed, can fully represent the consequences and efficacy of Christ's death."[1] Certainly the cross is a sacrifice, but it is more. We may add that its character as a royal conquest over sin has important implications for Christian life, for it points us beyond unresolved tension and dialectic conflict towards a positive and victorious life. "We have need that the death and passion of our Lord Jesus Christ should produce its fruit in us."[2] We are not only forgiven; we are to share in the conquest of sin.

(2) *Christ our Ruler*

The conquest of the Cross, however, is but the beginning of His reign, for Christ is the Protector of His people.[3] He is our Captain and Governor[4] who keeps vigilant watch over His people, who is ever quick to deliver them and to strengthen them in time of danger, for the kingdom "is never without enemies in this world. . . . It is well for us that our King, who lifts up His hand as a shield before us to defend us, is stronger than all."[5] Still more is Christ our "Shepherd," for this name better than any other suggests the loving patience and care with which He guards His people. "Nothing can exceed the kindness and gentleness of Christ toward the faithful, as He performs the office of a Shepherd; and He prefers to be adorned

---

[1] Comm. Eph. v. 2.
[2] Seventh Sermon on Isa. liii., *C. O.* 35, p. 676.
[3] Cf. Seventh Homily on 1 Sam. ii. 10, *C. O.* 29, p. 314.
[4] Comm. Acts xiii. 16.   [5] Comm. Ps. xxi. 8.

with this title, rather than to be called and deemed a king."¹

Christ rules His Church by His Word. "When all with one consent obey Christ and submit to His bidding (*pendebat ab ejus nutu*—hang on his nod), and how Christ designs to rule in His church we know: for the sceptre of His kingdom is the gospel . . . for it is not enough that Christ should be given as a king, and set over men, unless they also embrace Him as their king, and with reverence receive Him. We now learn, that when we believe the gospel, we choose Christ for our king, as it were, by a voluntary consent."² His rule is a rule of love, not of coercion. Why, then, are we so slow to heed His rule, Calvin asks. Our own happiness depends upon it, for "peace exists among us just as far as the kingly power of Christ is acknowledged, and these two things have a mutual relation. Would that Christ reigned entirely in us! for then would peace have its perfect influence."³ The pity is, that the kingdom's reverses are not so much due to outside hostility as to our own indifference.⁴

(3) *Christ our Judge*

While Christ's rule is a dominion of holy love, while He is the good Shepherd, He is also the Judge. If men refuse to live under His love, they will have to live under His anger, for Christ comes as the divine

---

[1] Comm. Micah v. 4. Cf. *Inst.* II.15, where he also includes the Shepherd metaphor in his description of the kingly office.
[2] Comm. Hos. i. 11. [3] Comm. Isa. ii. 4.
[4] Cf. Comm. John xii. 13.

judgment as well as the divine grace. "So then, the kingdom of Christ extends, no doubt, to all men; but it brings salvation to none but the elect, who with voluntary obedience follow the voice of the Shepherd; for the others are compelled by violence to obey Him, till at length He utterly bruise them with his iron sceptre."[1]

Thus, for Calvin, the eschatological "woes" of Jesus, far from being superfluous, are essential to our understanding of the New Testament, just as the imprecatory psalms are not so much expressions of mistaken national spirit, but are related to the judgment of Christ. For Calvin, David speaks not as a private individual, but as God's anointed who typifies the messianic judgment.[2] David "thus resembled Christ, who gently allures all men to repentance, but breaks into pieces, with His iron rod, those who obstinately resist Him to the last."[3]

As is His kingly reign, Christ's judgment is both present and future. He conquered the powers of evil in His cross. He continues to conquer them through the gospel which, while gracious to the church, is a rod of

[1] Comm. John xvii. 2.
[2] Cf. Comm. Ps. xli. 10 f. Without seeking to minimise the problem of the mprecatory psalms, it is not out of place to suggest that in Hebert's *Throne of David*, Calvin's view finds support again. "It has seemed to many people shocking that the psalmist should so curse his enemies. ... But there come times in the world's history when satanic evil unmasks itself: ours is one of them. That psalmist too was one who had been brought up hard against the mystery of iniquity. We are not in a position to judge him. It may be that at the awful sight of evil his courage and his patience failed him; we cannot say. But however that may be, we know that our Lord came to closer grips than he with satanic wickedness, and did not lose His courage and His patience, but endured even unto death. In His mouth the imprecatory psalms are safe; His judgment is the truth." p. 255. (N. Y., Morehouse-Gorham, 1941). Permission to quote from Faber and Faber, London.
[3] Comm. Ps. xviii. 37.

iron to His enemies. He will conquer at the last and will then vindicate His triumph in the final judgment. "God's sacred barn-floor will not be perfectly cleansed before the last day, when Christ at His coming will cast out the chaff; but, He has already begun to do this by the doctrine of His gospel. . . ."[1]

(e) *Christ our Priest*

Redemption means the reconciliation of God as well as the dominion of God. Therefore Christ's priestly work is inseparable from His kingly role. "We are, therefore, worse than ungrateful, if we do not keep our senses fixed on the true High Priest, who is exhibited to us as our Propitiator, that by Him we may have free and ready access to the throne of the glory of God."[2]

(1) *Christ's atonement*

Christ has "abolished the figures of the law" because He fulfils in His own person everything that the former priesthood typified. He is priest, victim, and altar.

He is *priest*. It was as our Priest that He became one with us. "Because it behooved our High Priest, by His own experience, to learn what it is to succour the weak, Christ would undertake our infirmities that He might be the readier unto mutual passion (*ad sympathiam propensior*); in which part, also, there appeared a certain image of sinful nature."[3] To be sure, Calvin says, "the Son of God had no need of experience, that He might

[1] Comm. Ps. xv. 1.   [2] Comm. John xvi. 24.
[3] Comm. Rom viii. 3.

know the emotions of mercy, but we could not be persuaded that He is merciful and ready to help us, had He not become acquainted by experience with our miseries; but this, as in other things, has been as a favour given to us."[1] By His gracious self-identification with our miseries He inspires our confidence in His redemptive work. His suffering had both a "proximate and an ultimate cause"—that He might learn obedience and that He might be thus consecrated as a priest for our salvation.[2]

He is the *victim*. The former priesthood could only typify atonement through animal sacrifice, but Christ is the sacrifice. He is the Lamb of God. "He who was nailed to the cross is the only propitiatory sacrifice, by which all our guilt is removed."[3] Thus, when Paul speaks of the blood of Christ, he "does not exclude the other parts of our redemption, but rather under a part he comprehends the whole sum, and named the blood wherein we have our washing."[4]

He is the *altar*. Christ's sacrifice needs no other ground than His own person. He is not the expression of a principle of atonement, but is Himself the atonement. "Christ is the altar of God, and on Him we must offer, if we wish that God should accept our sacrifices."[5]

Aulén suggests that a substitutionary view of the cross so separates incarnation from atonement that it is no longer God who reconciles. While orthodox formulas

---

[1] Comm. Heb. ii. 17.   [2] Comm. Heb. v. 7.
[3] Comm. John i. 29.   [4] Comm. Rom. iii. 25.
[5] Comm. Isa. lx. 7.

of atonement have frequently merited this criticism, this is not true of the meaning of expiatory sacrifice, as Calvin understood it. In a sermon on Is. liii, Calvin develops the relation between the wrath and the love of God. If God had merely pardoned us without Christ interceding for us and giving Himself as our pledge, it could still be of little account, and we could still pay an easy lip service. But when we see that God did not spare His only Son, when we see that He had to cry out "My God, why hast Thou forsaken me"—when we see these things, it is impossible not to tremble and be filled with fear and wonder at such measureless love, unless indeed we are more hardened than stones.[1] In other words, God's wrath finds its deepest meaning and expression in the measureless sacrifice of His love. When all is said, Calvin would urge us to bow in mystery before the cross.

> "We may not know, we cannot tell,
> What pain He had to bear;
> We only know it was for us
> He hung and suffered there."

Calvin echoes the thought of the familiar hymn when he says, "No language, indeed, can fully represent the consequences and efficacy of Christ's death. This is the only price by which we are reconciled to God."[2]

---

[1] Third Sermon on Is. liii, *C. O.* 35, p. 625.
[2] Comm. Eph. v. 2.

(2) *Christ's intercession*

"There is a necessary connection between the two things, the sacrifice of the death of Christ, and His continual intercession (Rom. viii. 34). These are the two parts of His priesthood; for, when Christ is called our priest, it is in this sense, that He once made atonement for our sins by His death, that He might reconcile us to God; and now having entered into the sanctuary of heaven, He appears in the presence of the Father, in order to obtain grace for us, that we may be heard in His name."[1] His intercession is thus the guarantee of our salvation, and the basis of our confidence in prayer. The prayer of Christ is "a safe harbour, and whoever retreats into it is safe from all danger of shipwreck; for it is as if Christ had solemnly sworn that He will devote His care and diligence to our salvation."[2] Calvin illustrates beautifully the efficacy of Christ's intercession when describing the trial of Jesus before Pilate. There Jesus remained silent in order that ever after He might speak for us.[3]

It follows that if Christ's intercession is our confidence in prayer, to rely upon any other is to deny Christ. "And in what way is it that He is invoked throughout the papacy, except with doubt and distrust, inasmuch as they know nothing about the office of Jesus Christ as our Advocate and Intercessor, by whom we obtain our requests."[4] Similarly, Calvin holds that

[1] Comm. 1 Tim. ii. 6. [2] Comm. John xvii. 20.
[3] Comm. Matt. xxvii. 12. Cf. also Calvin's fourth Sermon on Isa. liii, C. O. 35, p. 638.
[4] *Letters*, vol. 1, p. 368.

the mass as a sacrifice is a denial of the priesthood of Christ.[1]

(*f*) *Christ the Revelation of God*

How does Calvin relate Christ as the revealer of God to the messianic work of redemption? In the preceding chapter we have seen that Calvin suggested one possible answer in his later dogmatics by adding a third messianic office of prophet. Protestant orthodoxy has followed this lead. Yet we have also seen that Calvin never really uses this suggestion. Our study of his commentaries and sermons has helped to explain why the *Institutes* leaves the triple formula hanging in the air, in that it does not spring from his own exposition of the scriptures. Manifestly, the messianic work of redemption remains for Calvin a regal and reconciling work of king and priest. Now, if the triple formula does not truly express Calvin's exegetical method, we still must discover what is his real answer.

It should be emphasised at the outset that Calvin does not limit revelation to *act* by minimising it as *word*. He would have little sympathy with some contemporary tendencies in this direction. On the contrary, he constantly speaks of Jesus as our teacher. The Father "committed to Him the office of a teacher,"[2] "the only teacher,"[3] "the Master and Teacher of the Church,"[4] He is then "the only teacher, the Prince of all the prophets,"[5] He is "chief

[1] Comm. Ps. li. 9. [2] Comm. John viii. 26.
[3] Comm. John xiii. 20. [4] Comm. John xv. 15.
[5] Comm. Matt. xii. 42. Cf. also Sermon XXXI on the Gospels, *C. O.* 46, p. 380.

98 DOCTRINE OF THE WORK OF CHRIST

of the prophets,"[1] "He is head of all the prophets."[2]

To understand such phrases, however, two things need to be remembered. First of all, we must recall Calvin's free use of the word "office."[3] In the second place, we must remember Calvin's understanding of the place and purpose of prophecy. The prophets of the Old Testament are the interpreters of the law. "So it is seen that the office of the prophets was not only to predict things to come, but also to give good instruction to the people, to exhort them to repentence, and to edify them in faith, so we see that the prophets not only said, 'this thing is going to happen,' but they ratified the covenant of God by which He had adopted the people of Israel, they announced the coming of the Redeemer on whom rested the expectation of all the children of God. And then they comforted the afflicted, telling them of the promises of God's grace, yet also they warned the people when the people disobeyed, they made known their faults and transgressions, they called sinners to the judgment of God to humble them. All these things constituted the office of prophets."[4] The prophet "is one who interprets and administers revelation."[5] The

[1] Comm. Tit. i. 1.
[2] Comm. Isa. lxi. 1. "Christ testifies that He has been anointed by God, in consequence of which He justly applies this prophecy to Himself; for He has exhibited clearly and openly what others have laid down in an obscure manner. But this is not inconsistent with the application of this statement to other prophets, whom the Lord has anointed; for they did not speak in their own name as individuals, or claim this authority for themselves, but were chiefly employed in pointing out the office of Christ, to whom belongs not only the publication of these things, but likewise, the accomplishment of them."
[3] So, for example, Calvin will speak of God as "undertaking the office of a teacher." Comm. John vi. 45.
[4] Fifth Sermon on Deut. xviii., C. O. 27, p. 529
[5] Comm. 1 Cor. xiv. 6.

point to be emphasised, however, is that the prophetic or teaching office nowhere in Calvin assumes a separate messianic function. The prophet's work was to interpret the law which carried within itself the two-fold messianic promise.

There is a deeper reason. For Calvin the Word of God is always a redemptive word. True knowledge of God always means commitment to God. Since redemption is a kingly and priestly work, its ministration through teaching must also have this double character. It is thus a *kingly* function. "Thus the gift of prophecy in Saul was a kind of mark of royalty; so that he might not ascend the throne without credentials."[1] It is also a *priestly* function, for "there is no priesthood without doctrine of teaching, and no priest except he who faithfully performs his office as a teacher."[2] "These two things are, as they say, inseparable—the office of the priesthood and teaching . . . we hence see that all this belongs peculiarly to the sacerdotal office."[3]

What is true of the old covenant is supremely true of the new. Christ's word is a *kingly* word. "For His throne or sceptre is nothing else but the doctrine of the gospel. Nor does His majesty shine elsewhere, nor His empire otherwise exist, than when all, from the highest to the lowest, hear His voice with the calm docility of sheep, and follow wherever He calls them."[4] "Let us then remember that the doctrine we receive from God is

---

[1] Comm. Num. xi. 24. The reference is to 1 Sam. x. 10. For the same emphasis, cf. homily on 1 Sam. ii. 10, *C. O.* 29, p. 314.

[2] Comm. Mal. ii. 9. [3] Comm. Mal. ii. 6.

[4] Preface to Comm. Dan.

as if a king were speaking, and we ought to tremble before Him; let us not only come as little children who receive their lesson under a teacher; but as great and small come to listen what God speaks, and let us hear Him in all humility."[1] Christ rules by the "sceptre of His word." And this word becomes a "rod of iron" that will break His enemies.

Yet Christ's word is also a *priestly* word. "Christ undertook the office of a teacher, and justly, because He was the great High Priest."[2] Since "the authority of the law and the priesthood is the same, Christ became not only a priest but also a lawgiver . . . that He might be the teacher and interpreter of the new covenant."[3]

We have already seen that Calvin interprets the important passage in Deut. xviii. 15 ("The Lord your God will raise up for you a prophet") as a promise of the continuing order of the ministry, rather than as a messianic prediction. Of course, Calvin adds, the New Testament will naturally apply this promise to Christ who is the fulfilment of all prophecies and who is "the head common to all, the master of the house."[4] But there is a great difference. The prophet comes with another's word. Jesus *is* the word. Commenting on Deuteronomy's closing eulogy of Moses ("there has not arisen a prophet since like Moses"), Calvin says, "We know then that Jesus Christ was not a simple prophet, but that He is the living God who has been manifested in the flesh."[5]

---

[1] Second Sermon on Deut. xxxiii. *C. O.* 29, p. 121.
[2] Comm. John vii. 14. [3] Comm. Heb. vii. 12.
[4] Second Sermon on Deut. xviii., *C. O.* 27, p. 501.
[5] Second Sermon on Deut. xxxiv., *C. O.* 29, p. 232.

We are now ready to sum up. The two-fold character of the prophetic (teaching) office points us to the two-fold character of revelation. Christ does not convey another's word—He is the word. He is not given a revelation—He is the revelation, the self-revealing one. He is the "wisdom of God," "the light of the world," "the sun of righteousness." This last phrase from Malachi is one of Calvin's favourite descriptions, appearing again and again in his dogmatics, commentaries, and sermons. Let us listen to his exposition:

"All these words show that Sun is a name appropriate to Christ, for God the Father has given a much clearer light in the person of Christ than formerly by the law, and by all the appendages of the law [i.e. the prophets]. And for this reason also is Christ called the light of the world; not that the fathers wandered as the blind in darkness, but that they were content with the dawn only, or with the moon and stars. We indeed know how obscure was the doctrine of the law, so that it may truly be said to be shadowy. When therefore the heavens became at length opened and clear by means of the gospel, it was through the rising of the Sun, which brought the full day, and hence it is the peculiar office of Christ to illuminate. And on this account it is said in the first chapter of John, that He was from the beginning the true light, which illuminates every man that cometh into the world, and yet that it was a light shining in darkness."[1]

[1] Comm. Mal. iv. 2.

God in Christ is the self-revealing one. Revelation is therefore a regal claim and a reconciling grace. In spite of the triple formula Calvin had suggested in his dogmatics, his exegesis finds a different and truer solution —namely, that Christ's revelatory character belong not under the *de officiis*, but under the *de persona*, permeating as it does both his kingly and priestly work, and providing the bond of union that unites these. Had Calvin here developed systematically his own biblical theology, I believe this would have been his answer. As it is, we have enough evidence to make a legitimate inference. While Calvin never minimises the teaching of Jesus or the importance of doctrine, he does not make of teaching a separate messianic work *alongside of* the two-fold work of redemption. For revelation does not become a knowledge-as-such (a gnosis); revelation is always a knowledge that redeems, a reconciling word, a saving word—hence, a kingly and priestly word. There is no "neutral" knowledge of God.

(g) Conclusion

Does Calvin's treatment of the offices of Christ make redemption a mechanical transaction devoid of mystical devotion? Wernle, for example, objects that for Calvin, faith in Christ gives "very little place to heart and feeling, and relies only on a reflective mind."[1] Such criticism forgets that in Calvin redemption is not only the work of Christ *for* us, but also *with* us and *in* us.

[1] Wernle, *Der Evangelische Glaube nach den Haupschrift der Reformatoren* (Tübingen, 1919), band III, p. 47.

Christ is *Lord and Brother*, for the redeemer is always the man Christ Jesus. "And, indeed, if this were deeply impressed on the hearts of all, that the Son of God holds out to us the hand of a brother, and that we are united to Him by the fellowship of our nature, in order that, out of our low condition, He may raise us to heaven; who would not choose to keep by this straight road, instead of wandering in uncertain and stormy paths."[1] In both offices Christ reveals Himself our Lord and Brother. "Our faith is so founded on Him that He still rules over us, that He is in such a way our Brother that He is yet our Lord, that He was so formed by God as man, that He nevertheless by His Spirit revives and restores all things as the eternal God."[2] So also in His priesthood, "Christ is a brother to us, not only on account of unity as to flesh and nature, but also by becoming a partaker of our infirmities, so that He is led, as it were formed, to show forbearance and kindness."[3] He is one *with* us.

But more, He is *Head of the Body*. He is *in* us, and carries on His kingly rule and priestly grace through His members. As members of His body we are "a royal priesthood." He shares with us His kingdom and His priesthood. His unction becomes ours—that is why we may be called "Christians." "For Jesus Christ was anointed so that we might be enriched with the blessings which were given to Him in all perfection; and that is why we bear the name 'Christians,' for He bears

---

[1] Comm. 1 Tim. ii. 5.   [2] Comm. Heb. iii. 3.
[3] Comm. Heb. v. 3.

the unction."[1] All that Christ is, He wills to be *in* us. Calvin's letters reveal the warmth of his own faith. His theological affirmation is supplemented by the humble and earnest devotion of his prayers.

[1] Sermon on Luke ii. 26, *C. O.* 46, p. 372. The same exposition of the word "Christians" is made in his sermon on Luke ii. 9-14 (*C. O.* 18), and in Homily XXXII on 1 Sam. x. 1, *C. O.* 29, p. 592.

CHAPTER FOUR

POSTSCRIPT

(a) *Summary*

AS an attempt to relate and interpret the redemptive work of Christ, the traditional formula of the three offices has enjoyed a wide popularity. This popularity was due in the first instance to the influence of Calvin's *Institutes*. Yet the curious fact remains that the formula does not live up to its expectations in Calvin's own thought. Calvin began with the earlier and simpler doctrine of the two offices of priest and king. In this he was quite in accord with the prevailing exegesis and with the Reformation witness. If we try to account for the shift in his formal Christology we shall have to rely on inference, since Calvin himself neither calls attention to the change nor tells us why. It seems reasonably clear, however, that he added the office of prophet because it suggested to him a way of relating revelation and redemption, and because it suggested a foundation for the protestant ministerial order. The latter reason appears to me the stronger. Be that as it may, we have seen that the shift in Calvin's systematic formulation is an artificial change which does not find warrant in his own biblical theology.

Thus we are left with the odd fact that Calvin nowhere uses the formula that he had himself suggested.

This is true of the *Institutes* itself, and it is unmistakably apparent in his commentaries. "Whenever our salvation is treated of," he wrote, "let these two things be remembered, that we cannot be reckoned God's sons unless He freely expiate our sins and thus reconcile us to Himself, and then not unless He also rule us by His Spirit. Now we must hold, that what God hath joined, man ought not to separate."[1] In other words, revelation is not a "third something"; revelation is redemption since the Revealer is the Redeemer. Calvin is fond of describing Christ's word as His royal sceptre and His saving grace. What then is Christ's relation to the prophets? Commenting on Heb. i. 1, Calvin writes: "That we may understand this more clearly we must observe the contrast between each of these clauses. First, the Son of God is set in opposition to the prophets, then we to the fathers, and thirdly, the various and manifold modes of speaking which God has adopted as to the fathers, to the last revelation brought to us by Christ."[2]

In short, while the doctrine of the three offices historically may derive its popularity from Calvin, it is not an adequate or true expression of his own theology. In this instance the earlier and simpler formulation is the better expression of Calvin's Christology.

(b) *The Implications Tested*

Now, if the triple formula does not live up to expectations in Calvin, it may be allowed to raise the question of its validity and usefulness in general. I

[1] Comm. Ezek. xi. 19-20.   [2] Comm. Heb. i. 1.

would hold that the doctrine of the two offices of king and priest, a schema with which Calvin began and which he never really left, offers a more fruitful solution than does the *munus triplex*. It is, of course, quite beyond the scope of this essay to develop these implications exhaustively. However, it may be useful to relate our thesis to systematic theology by analysing briefly the nature of revelation, to biblical theology by checking our conclusions with accepted and scholarly findings in this field, and to practical theology by suggesting what it means in terms of the preaching of the gospel.

(1) *The nature of revelation*

Let it be said at once that if the "three offices" are used merely for cumulative or descriptive effect, there is little reason to quarrel. After all, what name shall the believer not ascribe to Jesus?

> "Dear Name, the Rock on which I build,
> My shield and hiding place . . .
> Jesus, my Shepherd, Brother, Friend,
> My Prophet, Priest, and King,
> My Lord, my Life, my Way, my End,
> Accept the praise I bring."[1]

What name shall I not give to Him whose name is above every name? "What language shall I borrow, to

---

[1] John Newton. I have used the reading common in American hymnals ("Jesus, my Shepherd, *Brother*, Friend"). The original, found in such hymnals as the *Scottish Psalter and Church Hymnary*, reads: "Jesus, my Shepherd, *Husband*, Friend." The variant itself illustrates the point I want to make.

thank thee, dearest Friend?" This is ever the spontaneous and adoring language of devotion.

On the other hand, it remains the task of systematic theology to find a prism that will adequately refract the myriad colours of the Redeemer's work. Here I believe the doctrine of the three offices is an embarrassment rather than help, while the double office illustrates and interprets the meaning of revelation.

After all, there is a duality in God's revelation. When God discloses Himself, He claims us and He condescends to us. He claims us, for He ever speaks as Lord: "I have called you, you are mine." The Name of God is the mark of ownership. In characteristic fashion the New Testament says the same of Jesus' name. "I bear branded on my body the owner's stamp of the Lord Jesus." (Gal. vi. 17, Moffatt). Indeed, the Apocalypse suggests that every man's forehead bears a name of lordship, be it the name of God and the Lamb *or* the mark of the beast. Revelation means that God speaks—as Lord.

Yet, paradoxically, revelation also means lowliness. God stoops to conquer. He whose ways are not our ways and whose thoughts are not our thoughts, He who "alone has immortality and dwells in unapproachable light, whom no man has ever seen or can see"—He speaks by coming to where we stand and by speaking in language that we can understand. For God to speak is for God to give Himself. If this is so, then the New Testament would rule out the possibility of a detached knowledge of God. To know God, to hear God, is to encounter God. The Gospel message is not a knowledge about redemption; it is redemptive knowledge. I cannot truly know about salvation without being caught up in the experience of salvation.

At this point the "prophetic office" of Christ embarrasses us if we try to place it "alongside of" the royal and priestly work of the Redeemer. To make Jesus a prophet who teaches about redemption has led orthodoxy into the perilous tendency of equating knowledge-about-redemption with redemption itself, substituting correct propositions about God for God Himself. On the other hand, it has led liberalism into an equally perilous tendency of making Jesus a teacher whose message can be disassociated from His person, a moralist rather than a saviour. In either direction there is the danger of substituting rationalism for faith. "The substitution of views for news", says James Stewart, "is one of the most damaging things that can happen to religion."[1] The crux of the matter lies here. "With your emphasis upon his statements alone," wrote Forsyth, "are you not in bondage to the bad old idea of revelation, namely, that it consists of a teaching rather than a person, of statement or precept rather than act, of a complete truth rather than upon a finished deed, of truth about God rather than of God as truth? How ineradicable, how subtile, that pagan, catholic, orthodox fallacy is!"[2]

(2) *The data of biblical theology*

Which systematic formula is closer to the data of scripture? However else the New Testament may understand and describe the work of Christ, it certainly

[1] James Stewart. *The Strong Name* (New York, Scribners, 1941), p. 95. Used by permission T. & T. Clark, Edinburgh.
[2] Forsyth, *op. cit.*, p. 119.

does so by relating the redemptive work to the messianic promise. For the New Testament the whole history of the Old is seen as messianic and redemptive in its ultimate thrust. Whatever may be said about their historical origins and developments, the two great institutions of the kingdom and the priesthood suggest from the outset a redemptive purpose, for Israel is to be a "kingdom of priests" (Ex. xix. 6). God is King, first through the theocracy, later through the Davidic king who, as the Lord's Anointed, becomes the idealised instrument of Jahweh's reign. The Son of David will not only reunite the scattered remnants of Israel and Judah, He will exercise more universal rule for God. "The government will be upon His shoulder." A. G. Hebert has nicely shown how the messianic promise, whether expressed in terms of king or city or age, is the central theme of the Old Testament.[1]

It may be objected that the priesthood is not given messianic treatment in the Old Testament. Certainly the high priest is not pictured as the Messiah. Yet the institution of priesthood points beyond itself and the ritual of the altar points to the need of atonement. It is not necessary (even were it possible) to picture the high priest of the Old Testament as a messianic figure. What matters is that the ritual of the temple and the sacrifice of the altar are fittingly appropriated by the New Testament to describe Jesus as "the Lamb of God that takes away the sin of the world." One does not need to turn only to the Epistle to the Hebrews to find this appropriation. The Fourth Gospel, for

[1] A. G. Hebert, *The Throne of David* (New York, Morehouse-Gorham, 1941).

example, continually shows how temple and ritual are fulfilled in the person of Jesus.[1]

And what of the mysterious figure of the Suffering Servant? Here is a separate, enigmatic, and tenuous strain in the promise. We shall not rehearse here the various attempts to identify the Servant by seeing an individual, a collective, or a fluid portrait. (Parenthetically, we may observe that the same fluidity marks the portrait of the Son of Man.) Many have identified the Servant as a prophetic figure, yet he is not pictured as a prophet. In a sense he dramatises in his own person what happens symbolically at the altar where innocence vicariously bears the cost of the guilty. "He makes himself an offering for sin" (Isa. liii. 10). I would call this priestly insofar as it appropriates the language of the altar. On the other hand, the portrait of the Servant is not wholly unrelated to the portrait of the Davidic Messiah, even though it would be illegitimate to suggest that this identification was made before the time of Jesus. However, both conceptions are drawn from common roots. Indeed, the Servant has some of the traits of the king, though not traits that belong so much to the regnant side of his office as to its other sides. "For there is evidence that the king played a part in the ritual usage of Israel."[2] One can see this usage, for example, in the Psalms. Rowley concludes that the evidence "would seem to justify the inference that the concepts of the Davidic Messiah and of the Suffering

[1] O. Cullmann, *Early Christian Worship*, trans. Todd and Torrance (Chicago, Henry Regnery, 1953).

[2] H. H. Rowley, *The Servant of the Lord and Other Essays on the Old Testament* (London, Lutterworth, 1952), p. 86.

Servant alike had their roots in the royal cultic rites."[1] If this suggestion is warranted, then the fusing together of these two concepts in the mind of our Lord was not without reason, however little this was anticipated in Judaism. To say this does not minimise the newness of Jesus' thought. It only suggests that our Lord was not doing violence to the two themes of Messiah and Servant when He brought them together in His conception of the Son of Man. Accordingly, it is truer to see in the Servant a fusing of "priestly" and "kingly" themes (using these words in the broadest sense) than to see him as an essentially prophetic herald. Whatever else he is, the Servant is a representative figure who "was numbered among the transgressors and bore the sin of many." So, at least, Jesus interprets the passage.

In post-exilic Judaism, as the monarchy recedes from the forefront of reality and expectation, the high priest begins to assume a greater idealised prominence. At first, the regent-king and priest are mentioned as equals (e.g. Zechariah's image of the two crowns, Zech. vi. 11-13). Soon, however, Zerubbabel drops from sight, while the high priest "acquired more and more importance as the person who was the upholder of the Israelite community."[2] One may add that the blending of kingly and priestly ideals finds a brief historical expression in the Maccabees.

Then came Jesus—no stereotyped figure but a living personality. He fits no preconceived patterns and breaks through all existing messianic expectations. He

[1] H. H. Rowley, *The Servant of the Lord and Other Essays on the Old Testament* (London, Lutterworth, 1952), p. 87.
[2] Pedersen, *Israel: Its Life and Culture*, III-IV (Copenhagen, Branner, 1947), p. 190.

transforms the Danielic "Son of Man" into a title that forever links the themes of Lord and Servant.

When, however, the New Testament seeks to interpret our Lord's mission, one can find evidence that the twin themes of Lord and Servant are drawn again in kingly and priestly terms. Christ is the priest after the order of Melchizidec. Hebert[1] points out that the Epistle to the Hebrews uses the shadowy Melchizidec pattern not so much because it has some anticipation in Psalm cx, as because the author has difficulty in finding apposite texts. After all, the Christian conception of priesthood depends upon the historical person of Jesus Himself, and neither John nor Paul had explicitly named Jesus as priest, though it is said that "He gave Himself up for us." Since the author of the Epistle is a theologian, he looked for a formula that would sum up the work of Christ, and this the Melchizidec figure provided him. We may add that the Apocalypse points to this same duality by picturing Jesus in high priestly garments, standing in the midst of the golden candlesticks, or again, as the Lamb in front of the throne.

Evidently, with all the names given Jesus in the New Testament, there are some indications of a theological attempt to see in His fulness two principal aspects. Christus Victor is Christus Immolatus. The new Israel, like the old, is to be a holy nation, a royal priesthood, an elect people (1 Pet. ii. 9). And this is possible only through Him "who loves us and has freed us from our sins by His blood and made us a kingdom, priests to His God and Father" (Rev. i. 5).

---

[1] Cf. A. G. Hebert. *The Authority of the Old Testament* (London, Faber and Faber, 1947), p. 213 f.

At this point it may be asked, is Jesus not our Teacher? If He is, why not apply to Him the title of "prophet"? In answering, we may notice that, although the title of "prophet" is given to Jesus in the New Testament, it is always with hesitation. Vincent Taylor puts the case in these words:

"The use of the phrase therefore in John and the Acts must be regarded as a limited attempt, in certain circles, at Christological interpretation, but one which proved abortive.... As in the use of the terms 'Rabbi' and 'Teacher,' we have in the titles 'Prophet' and 'the Prophet,' names which passed out of use because they were felt to be inadequate. Like the prophets of old, Jesus was seen to be filled with the Spirit and to speak the words of God, but unlike them, He left the abiding impression of possessing far more than the prophetic commission. In contrast with the formula, 'Thus saith the Lord,' there remained in the memory of the primitive community His majestic 'But I say unto you.' "[1]

If this is true of the witness of the primitive community, what of Jesus Himself? At best one could find two passages where Jesus refers to the title with reference to Himself, but neither quotation is decisive. Mark vi. 4

[1] Vincent Taylor, *The Names of Jesus* (New York, St. Martin's, 1953), pp. 16, 17. Used by permission of Macmillan & Co. Ltd., London. Cf. W. Manson, *Jesus the Messiah* (Phila., Westminster, 1946), pp. 18, 19: Manson points out how Apollos (Acts xviii. 28) and the Church at Ephesus (Acts xix. 1-7) had thought of Jesus as a prophet of the last things, but then passed from that imperfect witness to the confession of Messiahship. Such incidents, he suggests, may lie back of the question at Caesarea Philippi ("Some say one of the prophets") or such Johannine stories as the man born blind who first calls Jesus "a prophet" (John ix. 17), and then registers a higher verdict.

(parallels Matt xiii. 57, Luke iv. 24) reads, "A prophet is not without honour except in His own country." Here Jesus simply makes use of a common proverb to interpret the attitude of Nazareth. The second passage (Luke xiii. 33) reads, "It cannot be that a prophet should perish away from Jerusalem." Here again, Jesus is calling attention not to who He is, but to what Jerusalem is—the city that has always killed prophets and has been persistently deaf to God's voice. That this is the import of the saying is clear from what follows: "O Jerusalem, Jerusalem, killing the prophets and stoning those who are sent to you!"

William Manson has put the matter aptly:

"If anywhere the revelation of God in the Christian Redeemer asserts over us an entirely personal and unique ascendancy, it is in the domain where He is teacher. For here the starting-point is not a declaration of abstract truth but a particular, existential summons to our spirit, by which we are called primarily not to thought but to action, and to action vis-à-vis with God. In listening to Jesus we are not set in a situation in which to compare or contrast His teaching with other teaching—at least not for very long—or even to think of it primarily as a system of thought. We are brought face to face with *God*. . . . Something is wrought by this teaching as the result of which the hopes and ideals associated with religion are taken out of the realm of anticipation, in which they have hitherto existed, and enter on a crisis or actuality phase. 'The law and the prophets were until John.' "[1]

[1] From *Jesus The Messiah* by William Manson, Copyright, 1946, The Westminster Press, pp. 209-210. Used by permission.

All this is focused at the cross, for "all that Christ was in heaven or earth, was put into what He did there."[1] Even a chance reading of the Gospels makes this clear. Instinctively we know that the cross is central, it is "His hour." We recognise at once that no formulated theory of atonement can ever be wholly adequate. The biblical portrayal of the death of Jesus is so rich that a wide variety of theological expression could be regarded as true. However, if any structure can be found in the biblical language, I believe it will be that of the two offices. In the redemptive meaning of the cross we see most clearly the double thrust of revelation.

"This is Jesus the King." The sign of the cross was meant as a taunt, but it became a testimony. The cross is "His hour." Not all the forsakenness of Golgotha could take the victory from Him. "Be of good cheer, I have overcome the world." "It is finished." The New Testament often describes the cross as Christus Victor, because the New Testament ever views the cross in the light of the resurrection.

> "The powers of death have done their worst,
> But Christ their legions hath dispersed."

There is, however, another side to the cross. Christ gave Himself up for us. "Behold the Lamb of God that takes away the sin of the world." The cross is pardon. Put it into the language of satisfaction, penalty, sacrifice—put it into any words you will—the cross is self-offering. And here the language of the altar helps us. The cross is a priestly act. When Jesus died, the New

[1] Forsyth, *The Cruciality of the Cross* (London, Independent, 1948), p. 25.

Testament pictures the veil of the temple rent, for the sinner can now meet the holy God. It is scarcely necessary to enumerate the recurring emphasis on the "blood of Christ" as a covering for sin. "We are redeemed with the precious blood of Christ, as of a lamb without blemish and without spot" (1 Pet. i. 19). If Paul does not as often use metaphors drawn from ritual, it is surely plain that his own metaphors all point to that reality of propitiatory satisfaction which is essentially sacrificial in nature. We have always seen in some detail how the Epistle to the Hebrews is a theological attempt to interpret the work of Christ through the language of the ritual. All this is but to say that redemption is sacrificial in its nature.

Once again, it may be asked whether the cross is not also a prophetic sign. Does not the New Testament suggest that "Christ also suffered for you, leaving you an example?" (1 Pet. ii. 21).[1] Why not use the formula of the three offices? I think that the reason should now be clear. Revelation is not a "third something." Revelation is redemption. Revelation *does* something. The New Testament does not picture the cross as an object lesson. God in the cross is judging and justifying, ruling and reconciling. I cannot truly see the cross until I can say, "I have been crucified with Christ." To reduce the cross to an object lesson of God's love, Forsyth warns, would suggest that "God would be saying more than He

---

[1] It is apparent, of course, that First Peter does not develop an "exemplary" or subjective theory of atonement, for the epistle immediately reverts to the portrait of the Suffering Servant who "Himself bore our sins in his body on the tree that we might die to sin and live to righteousness. By his wounds you have been healed" (ii. 24). The epistle contrasts the prophets who prophesied of the grace with the Christ whose spirit indwelt them (i. 10-12).

did: and we have a natural and proper difficulty in thoroughly trusting people who say more than they do."[1]

In all this, we shall not suppose that any formula can embrace the fulness of the love of God in Christ. Here we would do well to follow Paul's example, as his theological passages spontaneously lapse into adoring prayer. "For this reason I bow my knees before the Father . . . to know the love of Christ which surpasses knowledge." Such recognition, however, will not excuse us from asking which Christological doctrine more adequately interprets this love, and which is in deeper accord with the biblical message. I believe the category of the two offices meets these conditions.

(3) *The preaching of the Gospel*

If the doctrine of the two offices, rather than the *munus triplex*, finds support in systematic and biblical theology, I would suggest that it also is more fruitful in practical theology. I realise that it is precisely in the realm of pastoral theology that the doctrine of the three offices has been most popular. (We may recall that Calvin's motives for the shift to the three offices were practical and pastoral.) It might be argued that the formula's practical value has long been established. How we do love trichotomy in sermons! How we revere the number "three"! How *convenient*, one might say, to embrace the meaning of Christ as teacher, saviour, and lord under the three offices.

However, if the triple formula is open to criticism on systematic and on biblical grounds, I do not see how it can claim practical usefulness. Not convenience, but

[1] Forsyth, *The Work of Christ* (London, Independent, 1946), p. 101.

accuracy, must guide our method. Nor have we the right just to assume its practical value.

If the Word of God is a "two-edged sword" that embodies God's power and pardon, ought not our pastoral expression to bear witness to this truth? It would appear to me that this awareness of the existential nature of listening to God's Word is not aided by a concept that makes revelation a precept rather than a person. If the sermon is the medium through which the living Christ can meet with man, let Christ be seen as the Revealing One. This is more than a quibble about words. It may well help us to spell out an epistemology that interprets the meaning of faith. In the double office of the Redeemer the possibility of detached and uncommitted knowledge is precluded. I believe that if this awareness characterises our preaching and teaching, the Gospel message will speak more forcibly to our time.

Simply put, it means that the preacher is the prophet. He does not bear his own word. He heralds the Word of God, the Word of judgment and salvation. Let the preacher rejoice that he may be the voice crying in the wilderness, "Prepare ye the way of the Lord. . . . Behold your God!" There are many voices; there is one Word, the Word made flesh. This is what Calvin meant when he called the preacher the *minister verbi divini*. This is what Paul meant when he said that Christ had sent him to preach the Gospel, "and to preach it with no fine rhetoric, lest the cross of Christ should lose its power! . . . For when the world with all its wisdom failed to know God in His wisdom, God resolved to save believers by the 'sheer folly' of the Christian message" (1 Cor. i. 17, 21, Moffatt). For ourselves and for others, the crucial question remains, "What will you then do with Jesus who is called the Christ?"

In John's vision of the City of God, there is a superb picture of the Lord of the years holding in His right hand the scroll of human destiny. The scroll was sealed, and no one was able to open it. John wept—and well he might, if the human story is forever to remain an enigma. Then he heard a voice say, "Weep not; the Lion of the tribe of Judah, the Root of David, has conquered, so that He can open the scroll." Great news! Good news! Then, as John looked to see this "Lion of the tribe of Judah," he saw standing before the throne of God "a Lamb standing as though it had been slain," while the chorus of the redeemed burst into song:

> "Worthy art thou to take the scroll and to open its seals, for thou wast slain and by thy blood didst ransom men for God from every tribe and tongue and people and nation, and hast made them a kingdom and priests to our God, and they shall reign on the earth." (Rev. v. 9-10.)

This is the paradox. The Lion *is* the Lamb. He is Jesus, the power and pardon of God. Lordship and lowliness have met in reconciling love.

The vision remains. The Church still lives to pray and sing and preach: Worthy is the Lamb, the Lamb upon His Throne! "Unto Him who loves us and has freed us from our sins by His blood and made us a kingdom, priests to His God and Father, to Him be glory and dominion for ever and ever. Amen."

you may also be interested in

Concerning the Eternal Predestination of God

by John Calvin
translated by J.K.S. Reid

Although he wrote comprehensively on a wide range of doctrinal issues, it is Predestination with which Calvin is most associated today. In this, his definitive text on the subject, he outlines fully a doctrine he feels has been wilfully misinterpreted to the detriment of the Church. Readers will witness Calvin masterfully arguing his points, wrestling with the scriptures, and fully engaging in the polemical world of sixteenth-century theological debate as he refutes the views of three of his chief detractors. J.K.S. Reid's widely praised translation preserves the nuances of Calvin's thought and the strength of his rhetoric, while his introduction offers a critical examination of Calvin's theological argument.

John Calvin (1509-1564) is widely considered the most important figure in the second generation of the Protestant Reformation. Having first encountered the ideas of Martin Luther while studying in Paris, he pursued the Reformed faith himself following a conversion experience in 1533. Eventually settling in Geneva, Calvin established a Protestant city government, while his landmark text, the Institutes of the Christian Religion, helped codify Protestant theology for Churches across Europe. Concerning the Eternal Predestination of God was published in 1552 after almost a decade of vigorous debate around the doctrine.

J.K.S. Reid (1910-2002) was a noted twentieth-century Scottish theologian. He was appointed Professor of Theology at the University of Leeds in 1952, and Professor of Systematic Theology at the University of Aberdeen in 1961. Alongside several monographs and significant ecumenical work, one of his chief accomplishments was co-founding with T.F. Torrance the Scottish Journal of Theology.

Expected 28 April 2022

Paperback ISBN: 978 0 227 17626 9
PDF ISBN: 978 0 227 90593 7
ePub ISBN: 978 0 227 90594 4

you may also be interested in

Image and Hope:
John Calvin and Karl Barth on Body, Soul and Life Everlasting

by Yaroslav Viazovski

Developments in biblical studies, neurosciences, and Christian philosophy of mind force theologians to reconsider the traditional concept of the immortal soul. At the same time, the concept itself tends to create axiological dualism between the body and the soul that in turn may lead to insufficient appreciation of the physical life in this world. A more holistic approach to the ontology of human beings is required. The aim of this study is to analyse the function of the concept of the soul in the dualistic anthropology of John Calvin and to compare it to the holistic anthropology of Karl Barth in order to answer the question of whether the transition from one to the other is possible without the loss of the functions fulfilled by the soul.

'*[Viazovski's] work helps to recognize Barth and Calvin in the historical continuum of Protestantism, without elevating them to dogma. For these reasons, Image and Hope deserves attention for those considering the Reformed tradition.*'
Joshua Kira, in Theologische Literaturzeitung

Yaroslav Viazovski (PhD, University of Aberdeen) is also the author of Karl Barth's Doubts about John Calvin's Assurance (2009).

Published 25 Fenruary 2016

Paperback ISBN: 978 0 227 17604 7

PDF ISBN: 978 0 227 90562 3

you may also be interested in

The Identity and the Life of the Church:
John Calvin's Ecclesiology in the Perspective of His Anthropology
by Yosep Kim

The Identity and the Life of the Church is a study of John Calvin's ecclesiology that argues that Calvin's idea of the twofold identity of the Church – its spiritual identity as the body of Christ and its functional identity as the mother of all believers – is closely related to his understanding of Christian identity and life, which are initiated and maintained by the grace of the triune God. The anthropological basis of Calvin's idea of the Church has not been examined fully, even though Calvin presents the important concepts of his ecclesiology in the light of his anthropological ideas. Yosep Kim provides an overall evaluation of Calvin's ecclesiology, arguing that it is ultimately Calvin's pastoral concern for the Christian and the Church under affliction that governs his theological understanding of the Church and shapes his proposals for establishing and sustaining the life of the Church in the world.

'A fascinating Study of Calvin's ecclesiology, focusing on the relation in his thought between the church's spiritual identity as the invisible body of Christ and her functional identity as the visible mother of all believers.'
Anthony N.S. Lane, London School of Theology

Yosep Kim (PhD, University of Cambridge) is Assistant Professor of Historical Theology at Chongshin Theological Seminary, Seoul, South Korea.

Published 25 December 2014

Paperback ISBN: 978 0 227 17456 2

PDF ISBN: 978 0 227 90266 0